URBAN DEVELOPMENT AND INFRASTRUCTURE

TECHNOLOGY AND THE FUTURE OF CITIES

OPPORTUNITIES AND RECOMMENDATIONS

URBAN DEVELOPMENT AND INFRASTRUCTURE

Additional books in this series can be found on Nova's website under the Series tab.

Additional e-books in this series can be found on Nova's website under the eBooks tab.

URBAN DEVELOPMENT AND INFRASTRUCTURE

TECHNOLOGY AND THE FUTURE OF CITIES

OPPORTUNITIES AND RECOMMENDATIONS

DIANA L. WASHINGTON
EDITOR

nova publishers
New York

Library of Congress Cataloging-in-Publication Data

ISBN: 978-1-53610-418-9

Published by Nova Science Publishers, Inc. † New York

CONTENTS

PREFACE

Cities are beginning a new era of change. From 1920 to 2010 many U.S. cities "hollowed out" as suburbs grew faster than their urban cores. The trend started reversing in 2011 as Millennials and Baby Boomers looking for social connections and convenience settled in urban neighborhoods. Accompanying the resurgence of residential cities are complex and persistent urban challenges, including resilience against climate change and natural disasters. This book focuses on the technologies that shape some key infrastructures and economic activities, as opposed to those involved in delivering education, health care, or social services. It also outlines a vision and an approach agencies can use to move forward together in pursuing a vision of smart and connected communities.

In: Technology and the Future of Cities
Editor: Diana L. Washington
ISBN: 978-1-53610-418-9

Chapter 1

REPORT TO THE PRESIDENT: TECHNOLOGY AND THE FUTURE OF CITIES[*]

President's Council of Advisors on Science and Technology

EXECUTIVE OFFICE OF THE PRESIDENT PRESIDENT'S COUNCIL OF ADVISORS ON SCIENCE AND TECHNOLOGY

President Barack Obama
The White House

Washington, D.C. 20502

Dear Mr. President:

We are pleased to send you this report, *Technology and the Future of Cities,* by your Council of Advisors on Science and Technology. It complements and goes beyond the ideas captured by the label, "Smart Cities,"

[*] This is an edited, reformatted and augmented version of a report issued by the Executive Office the President, February 2016.

identifying opportunities to improve people's lives both by modernizing key infrastructures (such as for energy, water, or transportation) and by using information technology (often with open data) to enhance city operations and services.

These opportunities illuminate new directions for place-based policy—investments to renew infrastructures will have greater payoff when they incorporate innovations rather than merely replace old and failing systems. Combined, the innovations that are increasingly within reach provide an opportunity to revamp how cities operate at all levels and for all stakeholders. Transforming cities around the world in this way is already a race—one that the United States cannot afford to lose. It is generating demand for new products, new companies, and new skilled jobs in the effort to produce the best urban environments.

This report drew from a working group composed of PCAST members and additional experts familiar with both key technologies and the evolution of cities and urban policy. It calls for a more integrated Federal approach to supporting new technologies in combination with a range of other innovations to improve the lives of city residents.

The urban ecosystem can benefit from the integration of a wide array of technologies that have been evolving rapidly, including systems to increase energy efficiency, renewable energy technologies, connected and autonomous vehicles, water and wastewater management systems, communications technologies to enhance connectivity, and new ways to do farming and manufacturing. The Federal Government can help to ensure a robust pipeline of such technologies for urban applications through improved coordination of relevant research and development activities, taking advantage of the National Science and Technology Council.

PCAST recommends interagency coordination in supporting experimentation with these concepts in discrete regions within cities (districts), using the competition/challenge model to motivate broad participation. It also recommends supporting and enlarging nascent efforts to share data and results from innovation, so that resource-limited cities can learn from each other as well as make sure that key insights are not trapped within a city silo.

The strategic orientation we advocate promises to connect the fruits of science and technology with the social and economic concerns that have long dominated urban policy. The time is ripe for an integrated approach to innovation to be brought to bear to improve the quality of life for all who live in cities, but perhaps above all the economically disadvantage and under-connected. PCAST hopes that the framework proposed in this latest report will help policy-makers at all levels to make the most of that potential. We are grateful for the opportunity to serve you and the Nation in this way.

Sincerely,

John P. Holdren
Co-Chair

Eric S. Lander
Co-Chair

EXECUTIVE SUMMARY

Cities are beginning a new era of change. From 1920 to 2010 many U.S. cities "hollowed out" as suburbs grew faster than their urban cores. The trend started reversing in 2011 as Millennials and Baby Boomers looking for social connections and convenience settled in urban neighborhoods. Accompanying the resurgence of residential cities are complex and persistent urban challenges, including resilience against climate change and natural disasters. This report focuses on the technologies that shape some key infrastructures and economic activities, as opposed to those involved in delivering education, health care, or social services. As described in Section 2 of the report, technological advances promise to improve the environments in which people live and the services that city governments and companies offer.

Cleaner energy technologies, new models of transportation, new kinds of water systems, building-construction innovation, low-water and soil-less agriculture, and clean and small-scale manufacturing are or will be available in the near future. These options, which are summarized in the Table of City Infrastructure Technologies, are evolving through private-sector commercialization and implementation plus university and National Laboratory research and development (R&D) in concert with city governments.

Information and communication technologies (ICT), the proliferation of sensors through the Internet of Things, and converging data standards are also combining to provide new possibilities for the physical management and the socioeconomic development of cities. Local governments are looking to data and analytics technologies for insight and are creating pilot projects to test ways to improve their services.

Technologies influence patterns of behavior. Digital and mobile technologies are making the connections between service providers and users tighter, faster, more personal, and more comprehensive. Sharing-economy business models are emerging that enable more efficient use of physical assets, such as cars or real estate, and provide new sources of income to city residents.

Large U.S. cities, through their Chief Technology Officers and related staff, are using technology and data analytics to solve specific problems in areas such as health, transportation, sanitation, public safety, economic development, sustainability, street maintenance, and resilience—problems that affect city residents every day. For example:

- The city of Los Angeles shares road closure, safety, and other data with app providers to improve driving, reduce congestion, and promote safety. In return, the app providers, such as Waze, share real-time crowd-sourced reports of issues encountered on the streets from more than 1.5 million users to the city's emergency management, police, fire, transportation, street services, sanitation, and other departments.
- The city of Chicago is working with the Argonne National Laboratory and the University of Chicago to deploy the Array of Things—a city-wide network of 500 lamppost-mounted sensors that monitor air quality, among other conditions; and it is analyzing its non-emergency complaint-call data to identify environmental issues such as pest infestations, connected to the incidence of asthma.
- The New York Fire Department started using data mining and predictive analytics to determine which of New York City's one million buildings are most likely to erupt in a major fire. They now examine 7,500 factors across 17 city-agency data streams and use artificial intelligence to track trends city-wide.

Because change in a city is costly (in many ways) and can be especially challenging for early adopters, it is important that the results of urban experimentation be shared, helping to foster less expensive and more easily replicable solutions. U.S. cities need a platform for collaborating with each other and all relevant stakeholders, sharing results, insights, and best practices. The platform should foster the development of standard, customizable models (for studying alternatives) and applications. It must also facilitate innovation from the bottom up, being neither built nor operated monolithically and, like the World Wide Web itself, having no central authority directing innovation.

This platform, beginnings of which already exist, is introduced in Section 3 and referred to as the "City Web." It can help cities build on each other's work and also open these solutions to smaller cities that lack the budget for significant technology capacity.

In this new era for cities, discrete and distinct districts and sub-centers are supplementing historic downtown centers—multiple areas within a city that provide either similar or complementary social and economic functions. Understanding and adjusting tradeoffs between physical and socioeconomic transformations in cities requires well-planned, integrated experimentation and implementation. That is difficult to do city-wide, but districts create the perfect living laboratory. A district does not necessarily have a predefined scale, nor must it fall within the political boundaries of a single city. A district has an area and population that are large enough for new technology implementations to have an impact, but also manageable from the point of view of clarity of intervention, tuning, collection of data, and assessment of progress and lessons learned.

The potential of a district-based approach first captured attention through Innovation Districts, which were primarily started to improve the local economy and create jobs in abandoned urban areas. Today technological implementations provide another path to impact, transforming city districts to become more energy-efficient and green; more convenient, accessible, and conducive to mobility; and more connected and inclusive. These goals are interconnected, and pursuing them jointly through integrated solutions can produce much more livable cities. For example, the use of connected and autonomous vehicles would greatly reduce the need for parking spaces and space dedicated to roads. Freed-up space could enable pedestrian paths, bike lanes, urban farming, and clean urban manufacturing; or it could facilitate change in the density of buildings, which might, in turn, facilitate the deployment of more-efficient energy and water systems, which could lower the cost of housing and help entice people back to the city.

In 2015, several Federal agencies, notably including the Departments of Commerce, Transportation, and Energy, started or increased efforts to implement programs of technology-based innovation for cities. A key milestone was the September 2015 announcement of the White House Smart Cities Initiative, which put a spotlight on the support for urban technology innovation being provided by a number of Federal agencies. It also featured the launch of the private, non-profit MetroLab Network, which pairs city governments with local university research labs using Federal R&D funding and philanthropic support to apply innovation to the solution of diverse city problems. And the Department of Transportation Smart City Challenge, launched in December 2015, has already inspired many cities to create innovative, multiple-stakeholder proposals in a competition for grant money.

Table of City Infrastructure Technologies

Urban Sector	Technologies / Concepts	Objectives
Transportation	Multi-modal integration via ICT applications and models On-demand digitally enabled transportation Design for biking and walking Electrification of motorized transportation Autonomous vehicles	Save time Comfort or productivity Low-cost mobility and universal access Reduced operating expenses to transportation providers Zero emissions, collisions, fatalities Noise reduction Lifestyles Tailored solutions for the underserved, disabled, and elderly
Energy	Distributed renewables Co-generation District heating and cooling Low-cost energy storage Smart-grids, micro-grids Energy-efficient lighting Advanced HVAC systems	Energy efficiency Zero air pollution Low noise Synergistic resource management with water and transportation Increased resilience against climate change and natural disasters
Building and Housing	New construction technologies and designs Life-course design and optimization Sensing and actuation for real-time space management Adaptive space design Financing, codes, and standards conducive to innovation	Affordable housing Healthy living and working environments Inexpensive innovation and entrepreneurial space Thermal comfort Increased resilience
Water	Integrated water systems design and management Local recycling Water efficiency via smart metering Re-use in buildings and districts	Active ecosystem integration Smart integration of water, sanitation, flood control, agriculture, and the environment as a system Increased resilience
Urban Manufacturing	High-tech, on-demand 3D printing Small batch manufacturing High-value added activities requiring human capital and design Innovation parks	New job creation Training and education Urban space conversion and re-use Close integration of living and work
Urban Farming	Urban agriculture and vertical farming	Lower water use Cleaner delivery Fresher produce

The rest of the world is not standing still. National governments in the United Kingdom, Germany, China, India, Brazil, and Singapore have stepped up with considerable organization and resources to become leaders in urban innovation, positioning their countries and companies for what is now recognized as a multi-trillion-dollar worldwide opportunity. Anticipating another 1.1 billion people moving into Asian cities in the next 20 years, the Asian Development Bank is allocating $18 billion per year in grants and loans to help transform cities. Other countries are also generating showcase innovations and, in so doing, improving the quality of life for some of their poorest people.

In reality, the nations of the world are in a race to transform their cities and reap the rewards, many of which will be economic—new products, new companies, and new skilled jobs, which, along with improved urban quality of life, create a virtuous circle that attracts talented new residents and additional businesses from around the world. This is a race the United States cannot afford to lose.

A Federal Government role is appropriate to ensure timely progress in a complicated arena rife with public goods. As the recommendations that follow indicate, that role involves the integration of many technologies, classes of stakeholders, and agency missions; facilitation of demonstration projects of a variety of kinds at district scale; coordination of interagency and public-private R&D investment; facilitation of new standards; workforce development; cooperation with state and local governments; and more. A more complete discussion of the recommendations summarized below can be found in Section 4.

Recommendations

The President's Council of Advisors on Science and Technology (PCAST) calls for the Federal Government to take a more integrated approach to supporting new technologies that can improve the lives of people in cities. Doing so would expand upon recent efforts to coordinate Federal support for individual cities. At the same time, a better-integrated Federal effort to encourage technological innovation in cities would support ongoing Federal programs that focus on economic disparities and physical infrastructure. A coordinated effort has the potential to:

1. Help the United States seize a new, multi-trillion-dollar business opportunity, including technology exports;
2. Create new jobs to support expanded development and implementation of the technologies discussed in this report and the revitalization of specific districts and ultimately larger areas of cities;
3. Enhance the quality of life for all city residents, in disadvantaged as well as more affluent areas, helping cities function better overall; and
4. Improve infrastructure that is critical for homeland security and for resilience to climate change and disasters.

Given the many Federal agencies with missions and programs that relate to cities, and the many opportunities to leverage one another's work, enhanced mechanisms for coordination of Federal activity are needed.

RECOMMENDATION 1. The Secretary of Commerce, working with the Secretaries of Housing and Urban Development, Transportation, and Energy, should establish an interagency initiative, the Cities Innovation Technology Investment Initiative (CITII), that will encourage, coordinate, and support efforts to pioneer new models for technology-enhanced cities incorporating measurable goals for inclusion and equity.

(1a) Under the leadership of the Department of Commerce, CITII should create and develop, by December 31, 2016, an initial blueprint for how U.S. agencies can foster systemic innovation across many dimensions of cities.

(1b) In advance of developing that blueprint, CITII should, through the use of competitions following the model of the Department of Transportation's Smart Cities Challenge, undertake activities to accelerate adoption of new technology. It should fund five districts with funding in the range of $30-40 million each, from existing sources in its constituent agencies, with at least two of the districts in low-income communities.

(1c) CITII should work with Federal agencies that have campuses that could be Federal "districts of experimentation," such as the Department of Defense with military bases, to create living trial/test-bed and demonstration areas that can serve as model districts. These collaborations would recognize and encourage innovation in natural/self-defined districts composed of single-owner campuses owned and/or operated by the Federal Government.

(1d)CITII, working in concert with the Department of Housing and Urban Development and the Department of Labor, should design training programs, including certificate programs, that can connect urban technology innovation to jobs development.

(1e)Under the guidance of CITII, the National Institute of Standards and Technology (NIST) and the National Science Foundation (NSF) should initiate a convening process to establish the prospects and parameters for an independent, community-driven body to define, implement, and evolve the City Web (a City Web Consortium), similar to the World Wide Web Consortium (W3C) and the Internet Engineering Task Force (IETF), which emphasize standardization based on broad adoption of common and proven approaches. The Federal Networking and Information Technology Research and Development (NITRD) program should work with CITII to coordinate existing activities to share data, models, and software tools among cities and stakeholders.

(1f) The U.S. Chief Data Scientist (CDS) should work with Federal agencies in CITII to identify types of data useful in the design and implementation of projects that improve public safety, public health, citizen mobility, and other desirable goals. The CDS should help the agencies promote new ways by which various stakeholders can develop and share best practices and data, attending to privacy and security. CITII should also develop a framework of incentives to motivate all stakeholders to share their data with others. This should include a common use-based model for ensuring privacy and ethical data use.

RECOMMENDATION 2. Because PCAST believes technology will play a crucial role in revitalizing low-income communities in cities across the United States, the Department of Housing and Urban Development (HUD) should embrace technological innovation as a key strategy for accomplishing its mission.

With its history in urban development, HUD should become an originator of new models for making cities more nimble and more adaptable to technological change. The Department will require the staff capacity and the funds on the scale necessary to support advances in urban technology and innovation. HUD should immediately appoint a Chief Technology Officer or Chief Innovation Officer. The Department should adjust future budget requests to establish programs such as innovation laboratories and other data and technology resources common to other agencies.

RECOMMENDATION 3. The Administration should seek legislation enabling two financing programs that will support cities and municipalities to develop Urban Development Districts (UDDs) and to introduce significant new technology in their communities.

(3a) The Administration should continue to seek approval by Congress of innovative new Qualified Public Infrastructure Bonds (QPIBs), which, as originally proposed by the Administration in January, 2015, would, if approved by Congress, provide an incentive for more private investment in technology-based innovation in cities. QPIBs extend benefits of municipal bonds to public-private partnerships.

(3b) The Department of the Treasury should create an Advanced Technology Infrastructure Incubator (ATII) Program. ATII would facilitate loan funding of technology-based innovation in Urban Development Districts at levels that allow for meaningful change and impact, particularly in low income districts. This would be scored, based on risk, by the Office of Management and Budget at an appropriate small fraction of the value loaned.

RECOMMENDATION 4. The National Science and Technology Council (NSTC) should create the Urban Science Technology Initiative (USTI) Subcommittee to coordinate Federally funded research and development (R&D). Building on more limited coordination efforts such as those revolving around smart cities, USTI would connect different kinds of infrastructural and other physical technology R&D with data- and ICT-oriented R&D. USTI should begin its work by creating an inventory of relevant R&D projects and grant programs across all agencies. PCAST also recommends that the research work of USTI be informed by the implementation work of CITII, and vice versa, a process likely to be in place in the beginning through the participation of the same agencies in both interagency activities.

1. Introduction

Cities are entering a fourth stage of modern transformational change, shaped by technological innovation. The first stage came with the steam engine, the second with the electrical grid and reliable mass transit (e.g., subway systems), and the third with the personal automobile, which stimulated the growth of suburbs and in turn necessitated the creation of a network of highways. The new profession of urban planning also transformed and created the cities that we see today.[1] Today more than 80% of the population in the United States lives in large metropolitan areas, generating more than 90% of the country's GDP.

From 1920 to 2010, U.S. cities "hollowed out," with suburbs growing faster than their urban cores. Many cities in the United States were characterized by concentrations of urban poor in their centers as the more affluent residents moved to suburbs, where they relied heavily upon personal automobiles in their daily lives. The urban centers generally have had higher levels of crime, lower levels of employment and income, deteriorating services, and often inadequate housing.

In 2011 the flight from the cities began to reverse, with Millennials and Baby Boomers leading the return to urban neighborhoods as they looked for social connections and societal services.[2,3] Cities are again growing. This fourth transformational era sees distinct districts and sub-centers supplementing unitary downtown centers. As a result demands on city design, infrastructure, and services are growing and changing. Important needs include more effective use of limited space, greater walkability, and ways to support residents across the income spectrum. In addition, the need for improved urban resilience in the face of climate change and other natural and man-made catastrophes adds to the challenges cities face. Integrating new physical and digital technologies to create innovative solutions will offer the best opportunities to address these challenges.

Viewing cities as collections of districts offers the opportunity to create both new, "green field" areas in cities and boldly reshape older, "brown field" ones. Both are evident in Detroit, for example, where the Detroit Future City Strategic Framework project addresses needs and anticipated progress toward revitalization through a series of maps that decompose the city into different kinds of districts,[4] while calling for them all to be sustainable, walkable, and conducive to mixed uses.

Against this backdrop, PCAST undertook this study to answer the question of **"how can the Federal Government best support science and technology and the related opportunities that can improve America's cities—in terms of quality of life, social services, infrastructure, and sustainability—for *all* their residents?"**

2. Current Activities and Near-Term Future Opportunities

Challenges faced by Americans living in cities are not new, but they are being exacerbated by city growth and aging infrastructure. They include the following:

- finding and acquiring a good job, a quality education, and appropriate training;
- accessing services and products such as health care, child care, and fresh food;
- living and working in safe and healthy environments;
- efficiently using energy for buildings and transportation; and
- reducing violence and insecurity.

These challenges are often intensified for those who are poor, disabled, young, alone, or aged. These same disadvantaged groups also often have the least opportunity to take direct advantage of new technologies so care must be taken to provide the best possible outcomes for all residents.

Advances in technology offer new approaches to addressing these challenges. Yet without help, many cities will be slow to realize the benefits of technology or may target investments in suboptimal ways. Cities need support to overcome a number of obstacles. Operating, maintaining, and financing existing services takes up the bulk of city governments' time, energy, and resources and forces upon them a focus on short-term efficiency, often at the expense of long-term innovation. Urban services are essential; people and organizations cannot function, much less reach their full potential, without reliable services and infrastructure. Yet the demand for stability inhibits exploration of options that deviate from proven practice, even those that promise to improve services, lower costs, or to provide other long-term and/or more equitably distributed benefits.

Other obstacles involve familiar challenges tied to obtaining resources. Subtler problems are often just as important, such as the lack of fluency within city agencies in the use of data and analytics that inform planning and decision-making, burdens from existing processes and regulations, mobilizing and coordinating different levels of government—from agencies to the Mayor's office within a city to metropolitan and State bodies that complement and sometimes constrain a city. Natural disasters such as Superstorm Sandy affect urban areas disproportionately; they also elicit the highest levels of coordination of planning and action across levels of government, given their urgency and the visibility of high levels of need. Finally, attracting, training, and retaining a workforce that is at once dedicated to the highest standards of public service and has the necessary technical skills to innovate is a perennial struggle for all city governments, especially in smaller cities.

Districts offer larger cities the chance to take on these challenges in bite-sized stages. Neighborhood councils, city-council districts, business improvement districts, tax districts, campuses (education, institutional, and commercial), Promise Zones, sanitation districts, and the many other forms of division and segmentation seen in the bigger cities make wide geographies and large constituencies manageable and serviceable. These districts are also a path to finding successful solutions that can then be extended to the larger area and population.

Though urban challenges are big, complex, and persistent, the opportunity is even bigger; technological advances staged through districts offer solutions to help cities become even better places to live, work, and visit.

2.1. Technologies Being Implemented Today and in the Near Future

Cleaner energy technologies, new models of transportation, new kinds of water systems, building-construction innovation, low-water and soil-less agriculture, and clean and small-scale manufacturing are or will be available in the near future. These trends are outlined in the Table of City Infrastructure Technologies and are evolving through private sector commercialization and implementation and university and National Laboratory research and development (R&D) in concert with city government.

Information and communication technologies (ICT), the proliferation of sensors (through the Internet of Things), converging data standards, and improvements in computational methods and technologies are also combining to provide new possibilities for the physical management and the socioeconomic development of cities. Local governments are looking to data and analytics technologies and creating pilot projects to improve their services.

Technologies also influence patterns of behavior. Digital and mobile technologies are making the connections between service providers and users tighter, faster, more personal, and more comprehensive. Sharing-economy business models, which can scale rapidly using the Internet to funnel excess capacity into exchanges for peer-topeer collaboration, are emerging. Those models enable more efficient use of physical assets, such as cars or real estate, while also providing new sources of income to city residents.

City services like education and health care are also profoundly changing due to technology. In the interests of confining the scope of this report to the use of technology for infrastructure, we do not describe those changes, which have been discussed in other reports by PCAST and other groups.

2.1.1. Transportation

Transportation in cities is on the verge of large-scale transformation, in part through the efforts by vehicle manufacturers, their principal suppliers, technology entities like Google, the Defense Advanced Research Projects Agency (DARPA), the Department of Transportation (DOT), and universities to develop connected and fully autonomous (i.e., self-driving) vehicles (CAVs), which are increasingly public and visible. These efforts are a natural evolution of the vehicle-safety features developed over many years into integrated systems with advanced software, data, and sensing. The potential cost savings to society and cities from CAVs, in particular, are significant. The cost of traffic collisions is approximately $300 billion per year.[5] Vehicular congestion costs the U.S. economy about $124 billion per year, with an additional $50-80 billion due to associated health-care costs.[6,7] The time regained from not driving is estimated to be worth $1.2 trillion per year; other benefits could come from repurposing land from dedicated rights of way and on-street and off-street parking spaces.[8] The application of shared CAV ownership models can transform land-use patterns in downtown cities to feature more bike lanes, wider sidewalks, or even more housing units by dramatically reducing parking requirements. An extreme example envisioned by Massachusetts Institute of Technology (MIT) researchers suggests that a fleet of shared CAVs in Singapore can nearly eliminate all parking and provide mobility to everyone in that city-state of approximately 4 million people, with an average wait time of 20 minutes during peak hours.[9] Depending on how they are implemented, CAVs also have the potential to dramatically reduce greenhouse gas emissions from personal and freight vehicles.[10]

Table of City Infrastructure Technologies

Urban Sector	Technologies / Concepts	Objectives
Transportation	Multi-modal integration via ICT applications and models On-demand digitally enabled transportation Design for biking and walking Electrification of motorized transportation Autonomous vehicles	Save time Comfort or productivity Low-cost mobility and universal access Reduced operating expenses to transportation providers Zero emissions, collisions, fatalities Noise reduction Lifestyles Tailored solutions for the underserved, disabled, and elderly
Energy	Distributed renewables Co-generation District heating and cooling Low-cost energy storage Smart-grids, micro-grids Energy-efficient lighting Advanced HVAC systems	Energy efficiency Zero air pollution Low noise Synergistic resource management with water and transportation Increased resilience against climate change and natural disasters
Building and Housing	New construction technologies and designs Life-course design and optimization Sensing and actuation for real-time space management Adaptive space design Financing, codes, and standards conducive to innovation	Affordable housing Healthy living and working environments Inexpensive innovation and entrepreneurial space Thermal comfort Increased resilience
Water	Integrated water systems design and management Local recycling Water efficiency via smart metering Re-use in buildings and districts	Active ecosystem integration Smart integration of water, sanitation, flood control, agriculture, and the environment as a system Increased resilience
Urban Manufacturing	High-tech, on-demand 3D printing Small batch manufacturing High-value added activities requiring human capital and design Innovation parks	New job creation Training and education Urban space conversion and re-use Close integration of living and work
Urban Farming	Urban agriculture and vertical farming	Lower water use Cleaner delivery Fresher produce

The development of CAVs is coming on the heels of a wave of innovation using apps, mobile devices, data, analytics, and the cloud to deliver new types of ridesharing, routing, cost avoidance, and market transparency. Apps such as Uber and Lyft are changing the need for privately owned vehicles. Waze, Apple Maps, and Google Maps are providing de facto load-balancing across entire transportation systems. Xerox and others are building mobility marketplaces, putting total trip cost, time, and environmental impact data into the hands of individuals at the relevant decision times. Automatic vehicle-location systems such as Nextrip are making public transportation more manageable by delivering real-time predictions and availability to riders. Many of these applications are enabled by a sharp increase in the availability of open data from transportation and transit agencies, with more than 80% of surveyed transit agencies providing some open data in 2015.[11]

Intelligent transportation system (ITS)[12] pilot programs are emerging throughout the world including experiments ongoing in Copenhagen, Helsinki, and London.[13] Singapore is already using autonomous vehicles, and Milton, a district of London, will start experimenting with them in 2016. Ann Arbor, Michigan has started using people-less transportation test beds with the hope of moving to real city district experiments with driverless cars within 6 years.[14]

Virtually all transportation technologies are introduced in geographic stages (de facto districts) that grow in size over time. Many people have suggested that CAVs, for example, will be offered within limited areas such as parks and campuses and grow organically from there to serve larger areas.

2.1.2. Energy

Increasing demand in the face of aging infrastructure has presented the United States and its cities with the opportunity to transform energy generation, storage, and distribution (as well as demand management). Energy systems involve a broad range of technologies including conversion systems (e.g., power plants, distributed renewables), transmission systems (e.g., power transmission lines, gas pipelines), and end-use systems (e.g., furnaces, boilers, air conditioners, heat pumps, lighting). Associated investments can also address issues of greenhouse-gas emissions, air pollution, reliability (including resilience following disasters), and cost and access for low-income communities.

Although energy systems are big, expensive, and long-lived, the growing trend towards electrification in cities offers remarkable possibilities for relatively rapid change. Electrification of many energy systems that currently involve natural gas or petroleum, such as building heating systems and personal transportation, is attractive for environmental reasons, but also may provide economic benefits. Efficiency gains and competitive pricing are being found in electric heat-pumps (for both heating and cooling) and in electric heaters with built-in thermal storage, which help manage the intermittency of renewable sources. Increasing numbers of electric vehicles that replace the same size and weight of internal combustion engines will require cities to plan for greater electricity demand with different time-of-use profiles, likely addressed through more efficient transmission, increased generation capacity, demand-side management, and distributed generation. However, through CAV technology the vehicles can be much lighter and smaller, with more variety, and can offset the electrical load with distributed generation.

Progress in ICT and monitoring systems offers opportunities to increase energy efficiency in urban buildings beyond what is available through traditional means alone, such as insulation or retrofits. Recent technical advances ranging from cooler LED lighting systems to better sensors and dynamic thermostats may dramatically lower energy demand in cities. Apartment buildings can be more efficiently heated by funneling waste heat from one unit to a neighboring unit. Today the lack of adequate control technology leads to very high heat loss from buildings; the simplest example is the tradition of opening windows to adjust heating levels. Buildings can also use smarter systems to manage their load, reducing peak demand charges and potentially providing gride services through demand-side management.

Moving beyond buildings to districts, the idea of "District Energy" matches local production with local use. District energy uses technologies to coordinate the production and supply of heat, cooling, domestic hot water and power to optimize energy efficiency and local resource use. Modern district-energy systems can also combine district heating with district cooling and thermal storage or with combined heat and power using heat pumps and water circulation, rather than steam.[15] For example, the Stanford Energy Systems Innovations (SESI) program represents a "transformation of university energy supply from 100 % fossil-fuel-based combined heat and power plant to grid-sourced electricity and a more efficient electric heat recovery system." It is a large district-scale example that employs the technology roadmap for building heating and cooling with thermal storage as recommended by the International Energy Agency.[16]

Three U.S. cities (Burlington, Vermont; Greensburg, Kansas; and Aspen, Colorado) are using energy technologies to declare themselves 100% renewable-energy cities in 2015;[17] these cities are using combinations of hydropower, wind, biomass, and solar. The city of Portland, Oregon became the first U.S. city to use a municipal water system to create renewable energy, using gravity to feed water inside the city-owned pipeline to spin turbines to produce the electricity for 150 homes in a collaboration of the water bureau with the electric utility.[18]

A plethora of energy-storage projects are being implemented in city districts around the world, including Detroit, the area around a group of 25 North Carolina State government buildings, and Albuquerque, New Mexico.[19] Additionally, distributed generation and electricity storage offer increased resilience to cities from natural disasters.

2.1.3. Buildings and Housing

The building industry has new options that, especially when adopted in an integrated manner, can make new construction scalable, cheaper to build, more energy-efficient to operate, and faster to complete. The opportunity areas include: (1) pre-fabrication, (2) modular construction, (3) customization and personalization, and (4) technologies for sensing and actuation. Pre-fabrication methodologies have many advantages over in-situ construction, such as higher precision, lower cost, and faster speed of construction. Used primarily for commercial buildings, pre-fabrication in U.S. housing lags significantly behind Japan and Scandinavia. Modular construction techniques involve the standardization of interfaces between building components. This enables the fabrication of a structural "chassis" that includes all critical subsystems (HVAC, electricity, etc.) and that can be prefabricated and assembled on-site, with snap-on elements such as exterior building panels and interior elements (including furniture) that can plug into the chassis. The ability to personalize the "infill" enables customizability to specific user needs, avoiding the failure of past (e.g., in the 1960s) one-size-fits-all modular home construction. Finally, the integration of sophisticated sensing and actuation technologies for building-systems control will enable the benefits of understanding and responding to changing environmental conditions and the dynamic needs of the occupants. The integration of these four areas can enable a new planning and construction process that is more coordinated and timely, more personalizable, reconfigurable, quick to deploy and construct, yields higher-quality construction, and scalable to non-residential construction like commercial, institutional, and industrial buildings.

The C40 Cities Climate Leadership Group, which includes 80 of the world's cities, representing 550 million people and one quarter of the global economy, recently did a survey that showed that 67% of cities have made a commitment to green-building codes and have 5,000 certified Leadership in Energy and Environmental Design (LEED)[20] projects, 61% have enacted municipal green-building codes, and 73% have green-school policies in place. Together with the U.S. Green Building Council and World Green Building Council, they created a compendium of leading efforts of 67 cities worldwide, but only 12 such cities were in the United States.[21] Austin, Texas established the first municipally operated green-building program in the world in 1990, created the United States' first green-building rating system for homes in 1991, and established the goal, by a city council-passed resolution, to reach net-zero community greenhouse gas emissions by 2050.[22]

2.1.4. Water

The useful life of much of today's water infrastructures is ending.[23] This situation offers the opportunity to investigate the creation of integrated water networks using an ecosystem approach incorporating water, sanitation, flood control, agricultural, and environmental needs at regional, watershed, and local levels. Demand on traditional large-scale water infrastructure can be reduced by increasing reliance on local solutions. Local investments in storm-water capture, recycling and reuse, groundwater management, and conservation can dramatically reduce water imports in a particular geographic area.

The 2013 update of the Greater Los Angeles County Integrated Regional Water Management plan included a twenty-year plan to meet the region's water supply needs. The largest changing component is storm-water capture. By appending single household and district-level (neighborhood) storm-water capture systems to the traditional regional ones, Los Angeles could further triple or quadruple its expected storm-water capture by 2099.[24] One such neighborhood-scale storm-water capture system in development is the Rory M. Shaw Wetlands Park in Los Angeles, which converts a 46-acre landfill site into a storm-water capture facility and multipurpose park. The treated storm-water is piped to adjacent infiltration basins.[25] Similar "blue" (water-related) projects are planned for Detroit.[26]

Neighborhood (district) storm-water storage systems can also be deployed to reduce the amount of water treated to drinking water standards when that water could instead be used for other purposes. In the Saint Anthony Village district of Minneapolis, a half-million-gallon storm-water storage reservoir lies below an attractive pond with fountains. Since that water can be used locally for field irrigation, or washing of the grandstands at the local ballpark, it can dramatically save money by obviating treatments that would otherwise be used at regional level to create potable water and reduce phosphorus discharges to surface water that would occur in the treatment process.[27]

2.1.5. Urban Farming

New approaches to urban farming featuring soil-less (hydroponic, aquaponic, aeroponic) systems are deployed into greenhouses, rooftops, and building interiors and even integrated into façades of buildings. These offer glimpses of significant positive impact (lowering the cost and increasing availability of fresh food) when scaled to industrial levels of food production. NASA demonstrated aeroponic farming on the Mir space station to test food growth under scarce water conditions in orbit. Periodic misting of plant roots saved up to 98% of the water and 60% of the nutrients required of soil-based farming.[28] In addition, urban farming using compost closes the waste cycle and creates an effective carbon sequestration cycle.

Urban agriculture is reviving the Ironbound district in Newark. Aerofarms[29] converted a steel plant into an indoor vertical farm that uses aeroponics to create two million pounds of lettuce a year in 30 harvests sold to local grocery stores, restaurants, and schools.[30]

Rooftop greenhouses are yielding year-round, local premium quality produce under the highest standards of food safety and environmental sustainability in Queens, Brooklyn, and Chicago. An advanced greenhouse in the Pullman district in Chicago's south side is comprised of 75,000 square feet growing 10 million heads of leafy greens and herbs per year on a rooftop. It is also the world's first LEED-Platinum certified manufacturing plant in its industry.[31]

2.1.6. Urban Manufacturing

Small urban manufacturers make a wide variety of specialized products, including sophisticated medical equipment, designer coats, or artisanal food products. They serve a spectrum of customers and markets, including small suppliers, contractors, large original equipment manufacturers (OEMs), and the general public. Manufacturing of new technologies can support higher median wages, and open up opportunities for jobs of every level and skill. Manufacturing jobs pay an average of over $50,000 in comparison to retail or industrial jobs that can range from $25,000-38,000.[32]

These new technologies are cleaner than their predecessors and enable the development of neighborhoods where factories are built next to housing and transportation. For example, the Fremont, California Tesla auto plant will be built in a dense mixed-use residential, commercial, and retail district; there are also plans for the plant to have a new commuter train station built next to it.[33] This new face of urban manufacturing is part of the "Maker Movement" that is helping redefine employment and foster inclusive, connected cities.

The Equitable Innovation Economies Initiative (EIE) is an example of an effort aimed at capitalizing on the growth of high–tech industries and innovation to create opportunities for low-income and underserved communities.[34] This three-year project was launched by the Pratt Center for Community Development in collaboration with the Urban Manufacturing Alliance (UMA) and PolicyLink. Four cities (New York City, Indianapolis, Portland, and San Jose) have been selected to develop a community of practice to enable cities to address issues and challenges related to development of innovation-based economic activities, reframe economic development strategies, share best practices, and provide a database to compare economic development efforts in advancing equity.

There are efforts under way to create distributed urban supply-chain management through the integration of an entire region's set of manufacturers, logistics services, energy providers, and transportation systems to optimize at a level beyond what has been done to date within companies, product lines, or manufacturing lines. These build upon traditional manufacturing districts, such as the toy district and the garment district in Los Angeles.

2.2. Transformations Happening in Urban Development Districts

Understanding and adjusting tradeoffs between physical and socioeconomic transformations in cities requires well planned, integrated experimentation and implementation. That is difficult to do city-wide and much easier to do in a smaller area of a city. Districts are called many things and organized in many ways; a district does not necessarily have a predefined scale, nor must it fall within the political boundaries of a single city. For purposes of this discussion, a district has an area and population that are large enough for new technology implementations to have an impact, but also manageable from the point of view of clarity of intervention, tuning, collection of data, and assessment of progress and lessons learned.

The potential of a district-based approach first captured attention through "Innovation Districts." These were primarily started to improve the local economy and create jobs in abandoned urban areas. According to a recent Brookings Institution report,[35] Innovation Districts:

1. Enabled cities to grow jobs through the embracing of disruptive technology;
2. Empowered entrepreneurs and start-up companies to use shared spaces to increase collaboration with mentors and investors and reduce overhead costs;
3. Provided improvements in infrastructure, education, and public space to the benefit of adjacent neighborhoods that were typically low-to-middle income neighborhoods; and
4. Created revenue that helped improve the adjacent infrastructure, housing, public safety, schools, and other services.

Today technological implementations are also "re-platforming" districts to become more energy-efficient or green, convenient and accessible or mobile, and connected or inclusive. These goals are interconnected, and they also involve the integration of distinct technologies and policies. We summarize in the Table of Three Key Dimensions some of the characteristics of these three dimensions being implemented today.

In contrast to simpler first-generation Innovation Districts, we refer to these potential new districts as "Urban Development Districts" (UDDs). They are living laboratories from which fundamental knowledge about urban processes and practical implementation practices can be learned, adapted, and generalized to other districts, recognizing that they will differ in many ways, such as new versus retrofit construction, warm versus cold climates, or congested versus open transportation routes.

The greatest impact comes from the integration of technologies to optimize a district. For example, the use of autonomous vehicles would greatly reduce the need for parking spaces and space dedicated to roads. Freed-up space can make possible pedestrian paths, bike lanes, urban farming and manufacturing, or a different density of buildings, which may change the energy or water systems deployed, which could lower the cost of housing and entice migration back to the city. Cities can combine the technologies, build and calibrate models, simulate interventions, and deploy actual technology pilots in UDDs. They can share the results, insights, and algorithms within the city and with other cities.

Table of Three Key Dimensions

	Efficient / Green	**Convenient / Mobile**	**Connected**
Socioeconomic issues	Clean air Clean water Comfortable and affordable living	Safer neighborhoods Affordable transportation	Better education and training Social capital Poverty elimination
Transport	Reduce CO_2 Reduce pollution Reduce noise Improve land uses	Increase walkability Decrease vehicular congestion Eliminate traffic fatalities	Universal access Reduce time Increase health comfort and productivity
Buildings	Reduce CO_2 Reduce energy use	Comfort Home management	Health living and working environments Affordable housing Safety
Water	Efficient consumption Storm water management Recycling		Access to water
Health	Reduce asthma cases	Access to hospitals	Affordable and accessible health care Eliminate food deserts
Energy	Implement smart grid	Diminished energy transport	Universal access Reliability Human capital

2.2.1. Energy-Efficient "Green" Districts

"Green" districts use design principles and technologies to create dense, mixed-use areas, typically using renewable energy sources. Various metrics are being considered to gauge success. The U.S. Green Building Council has extended its LEED rating system for individual buildings to a LEED for Neighborhood Development (LEED-ND), which applies to a kind of district and rewards reducing sprawl in housing development.[36] More than 300 projects have earned the LEED-ND rating. In June 2014, the Clinton Global Initiative and EcoDistricts, an independent group funded by six foundations, began the Target Cities program to create energy-efficient, resilient, and sustainable, neighborhoods. Today, EcoDistricts is helping with pilot projects in 11 North American communities.[37] For example, one of their projects is the Downtown Business Improvement District (BID) of Washington, D.C., a 138-block area that has set a goal to reduce the district's energy consumption by 20% by 2020. Downtown BID has identified transit, LEED certifications and registrations, green-power purchasing, and Energy Star programs as some of the priority projects. Another, the Seaholm District of Austin, Texas is an 85-acre redevelopment area on the southwestern edge of downtown Austin, including the redevelopment of the Art Deco-style Seaholm Power Plant building to include major office and restaurant space and planned developments of 1,475 units of multi-family housing, offices, and retail; development in the area complies with LEED or Austin Energy Green Building criteria and features a new energy-efficient Downtown District Cooling System.

Green districts will continue to proliferate. Early experiments and models indicate they are economically viable, environmentally beneficial, and can improve health and quality of life. A recent McKinsey study looked at 25 building and energy technologies and concluded that, while construction costs were higher, operating costs were lower and payback was typically achieved in three to five years, while resulting in 20 to 40 percent lower energy consumption, 60 to 65 percent less freshwater consumption and wastewater production, 25 percent less solid waste going to the landfill, and 30-50% lower emissions.[38] Cities are setting climate goals around waste, clean transportation, and renewable energy, with visible annual incentives their departments. For example, San Francisco's climate goals are 0% waste, 50% of all travel by sustainable modes, and 100% renewable energy by 2025.[39]

Cities can work with local district residents to revitalize their own neighborhoods and to enable residents to become owners and developers themselves. For example, the "Green Healthy Neighborhoods" program in Chicago leveraged open data, community involvement, and city government cooperation to create the "Large Lots" program.[40] The program allows residents in some of Chicago's most distressed neighborhood areas to purchase vacant lots on their block for $1. Using open data and the principles of open APIs, civic technologists worked with community organizations, the city of Chicago, and Cook County to create a Web-based system that enables residents to find lots using an online map and to determine if they are eligible to purchase them, and then guides the resident through a complex set of county and city applications. Loveland Technologies, a company based in Detroit and San Francisco, has developed software to map every parcel of land in the

United States to understand usage. Loveland started in Detroit with an effort to fight blight by marking foreclosed properties.[41]

2.2.2. *Convenient, Accessible, "Mobile" Districts*

U.S. cities after World War II became increasingly dependent on cars and trucks as the primary means of transportation for people and goods.[42] Although more Americans use public transportation, walk, and bike than ever before, the shares of different types of transportation have remained remarkably stable since 1960. The convergence of several new technologies and of changing behavior has the ability to change this situation dramatically, especially by blurring the lines between different modes of transportation and disrupting associated economic models of ownership and public provision.[43] This creates new opportunities to re-think land use, improve environmental conditions, and foresee economic models for future transportation that can address many of the problems of the Nation's transportation infrastructure today. For example, in incorporated Los Angeles County, there are 18.6 million parking spaces accounting for 14% of all land, but the amount of space dedicated to parking in the central business district (including multi-level parking structures) in Los Angeles is a staggering 81%, and the numbers are also high in other cities—25% and 31% in Phoenix's and San Francisco's respective central business districts. It is estimated that more than 30% of San Francisco and Los Angeles traffic in the central business district is due to people looking for parking spaces. While the eventual application of shared and CAVs can have a most dramatic effect, current near-term ideas yielding more convenient, accessible, or mobile districts can greatly reduce private vehicle-miles traveled.[44]

Increasing walking and biking in cities represents an immediate and low-risk opportunity to reduce carbon emissions, energy and land consumption, and the cost of transportation in cities, while simultaneously improving the health and well-being of urban dwellers. The other benefits include increased social interaction and reduced crime (Jane Jacob's "eyes on the street effect").[45,46]

For example, the Seaholm district of Austin, Texas is implementing a new multi-modal transportation network with a planned Metro Rail stop, bus transit, bike sharing, car sharing, hike-and-bike trail connections, and a five-mile cross-city route connecting with the Lance Armstrong Bikeway.[47] The 42-acre Talbot Norfolk Triangle (TNT) neighborhood in Boston, a low-income community, recently opened Talbot Avenue Station along the Fairmount Corridor Line, providing a strong basis for increased density through transit oriented development (TOD).[48] Area residents taking advantage of the commuter rail line now reach downtown Boston in 20 minutes or less, a trip that takes 1.25-1.5 hours via bus, with both fewer vehicle miles travelled and increased walkability.

Table 3.

Top Ten Metro Areas for Commutes to Work by Bicycle: 2009

(Numbers in thousands. For information on confidentiality protection, sampling error, nonsampling error, and definitions, see *www.census.gov/acs/www/*)

Metropolitan statistical area	Commuted by bicycle[1]	
	Percent	Margin of error[2] (±)
Corvallis, OR	9.3	3.1
Eugene-Springfield, OR	6.0	1.2
Fort Collins-Loveland, CO	5.6	2.1
Boulder, CO	5.4	1.2
Missoula, MT	5.0	1.8
Santa Barbara-Santa Maria-Goleta, CA	4.0	0.9
Gainesville, FL	3.3	1.2
Logan, UT-ID	3.3	1.4
Chico, CA	3.0	1.2
Bellingham, WA	3.0	1.3

[1] Workers 16 years and over.

[2] This number, when added to or subtracted from the estimate, represents the 90 percent confidence interval around the estimate.

Note: Because of sampling error, the estimates in this table may not be significantly different from one another.

Source: U.S. Census Bureau, American Community Survey, 2009.

Table 4.

Top Ten Metro Areas for Commutes to Work by Walking: 2009

(Numbers in thousands. For information on confidentiality protection, sampling error, nonsampling error, and definitions, see *www.census.gov/acs/www/*)

Metropolitan statistical area	Walked to work[1]	
	Percent	Margin of error[2] (±)
Ithaca, NY	15.1	3.2
Corvallis, OR	11.2	3.0
Ames, IA	10.4	2.9
Champaign-Urbana, IL	9.0	1.5
Manhattan, KS	8.5	2.4
Ocean City, NJ	8.4	2.9
Iowa City, IA	8.2	1.4
Hinesville-Fort Stewart, GA	8.2	5.1
Jacksonville, NC	8.1	3.0
State College, PA	8.0	2.0

[1] Workers 16 years and over.

[2] This number, when added to or subtracted from the estimate, represents the 90 percent confidence interval around the estimate.

Note: Because of sampling error, the estimates in this table may not be significantly different from one another.

Source: U.S. Census Bureau, American Community Survey, 2009.

New planned TODs like TNT with mixed-use zoning as well as the emergence of smart-phone enabled on-demand services with flexible routing that employ smaller vehicles (shuttles, vans, etc.) can alleviate automobile usage and augment mass transit needs with less investment and higher levels of demand responsiveness. Currently these systems are run by private industry (Uber, Lyft, Bridj), but public-private partnerships could leverage existing mass-transit systems, extending the benefits to lower-income residents. Finding ways for cities to motivate private sector companies to share transit data can be most helpful in next generation city planning.

2.2.3. Connected, "Inclusive" Districts

Districts can use technologies from broadband access to transportation to more affordable or multi-use housing to help people be more connected to each other and to economic activity. Technology can help districts to be more equitable and inclusive as long as those goals are built in from the beginning and equity metrics are used as part of the measurement of success.

For example, technology can be applied in UDDs to greatly enhance the lives of an aging population of individuals over the age of 60, a demographic category expected to double by 2050 with a majority living in cities. Older people are more vulnerable to environmental pollutants, especially airborne particulates, and respiratory conditions, such as chronic obstructive lung disease, are common for this population and can lead to disability, limited ability to be outside and to exercise, and hospitalizations. Many older adults have diminishing abilities to drive; available and affordable alternatives allow them to maintain their independence. Social engagement as people age helps to maintain cognitive capacities and prevent depression, a significant (30% prevalence in older adults) and debilitating disorder that is both preventable and treatable. Where physical mobility is limited, Internet-mediated communications and health monitoring strengthen families, create opportunities for interaction with others, and allow older persons to continue to live independently while being in close touch with family. High-density living arrangements offer features that are consistent with preferences of Millennials as well as aging Baby Boomers, and addressing such risks as crime while enhancing the advantages such as mobility management and shared transportation benefits all age groups. A further analysis of this is presented in Appendix F. PCAST has completed a report on how technology can help people maintain their independence as they age.[49]

2.3. Data-Enabled Pilot Projects Being Implemented by City Chief Technology Officers

Mapping technologies applicable to cities to actual urban challenges requires moving from science-based research and development to human-focused use cases. Cities are using sensors (often crowd-sourced) and real-time data to solve specific problems in domains such as health, transportation, sanitation, public safety, economic development, sustainability, street maintenance, and resilience. Pilot projects are showing the usefulness of sharing across city-agency and private-sector silos and of new kinds of analytics. Sophisticated use of data also allows cities to set more aggressive future metric goals. A number of forward-looking city plans involving sustainability and resilience rely upon advances in technology and data analytics that are only now emerging. A few example pilot projects occurring in cities worldwide are briefly described in the table below and expanded upon in Appendix B.

Table of Example Data-Enabled Pilot Projects

Focus Area	Program descriptions
Public Health and Asthma	Several cities are developing strategies based on new technologies and data that allow them to track the challenges experienced by patients and identify more proximate causes of this common health challenge.
	Pittsburgh – Breathe Cam[50]
	Detroit, Los Angeles, Lowell (MA), Boston, and NYC – hospital-admissions data to identify areas with the highest incidence of asthma[51]
	Louisville, KY with IBM Smart Cities and Propeller Health – free GPS sensor and phone app for their inhalers[52]
	Chicago – Array of Things, analyzing non-emergency complain call data to identify environmental issues[53]
Reducing Air Pollution	Some basic tools have been developed associated with the emerging *Global Protocol for Community-Scale Greenhouse Gas Emission Inventories (GPC),*[54] developed under the recent agreement known as the *Compact of Mayors.*[55]
Eliminating Deaths and Serious Injuries on the City's Streets	Data and analysis offer cities means to reduce the dangers of automobile-based transportation systems. Often referred to as Vision Zero, the idea can be summed up as, "when a child runs after a bouncing ball into a residential street and a speeding car strikes and kills him, the Vision Zero philosophy maintains [that] the death shouldn't be seen as an unavoidable tragedy but as the result of an error of road design or behavioral reinforcement, or both."[56]

Focus Area	Program descriptions
	• San Francisco, New York City, Los Angeles, Washington, D.C. – Vision Zero[57] • Los Angeles – High Injury Network and Safe Routes to School[58]
Fire Prevention	The New York Fire Department (NYFD) started using data mining and predictive analytics to determine which buildings are most likely to erupt in a major fire. Roughly 60 different factors have been built into an algorithm that assigns each of the inspect-able buildings with a risk score. The risk score now determines the order of inspection, as opposed to a process that returns to previously inspected buildings randomly or based on safety priorities.[59]
Street Services	The city of Los Angeles is currently in the process of adding Global Positioning Systems, sensors, and cameras to their street sweepers. This will allow the city to open streets for parking more quickly, track water usage, tune or change routes to real-time priorities, and track coverage to make sure street sweeping is complete.[60]
Recycling	The city of Los Angeles is rolling out a franchise-management system to integrate private waste companies into the cities' system of service calls, data tracking, and billing to work together to deliver yard waste services to multi-unit dwellings and commercial locations.[61]
Load-Balancing of Street Systems	A number of apps have been published that let drivers and passengers identify shortest routes over city streets. Cities are sharing real-time data with these apps, and receiving reports from them, in an effort to optimize the use and management of city streets. • Country wide – Waze • Denver, Los Angeles – CitySight[62]
Energy	Envision Charlotte uses smart meters to monitor the energy use of 61 buildings. Stanford and other universities are doing campus-wide energy management through smart meters and local energy management.[63]

2.4. The Emerging Urban Science Profession and Degrees

As cities increase in complexity, the need for professional management increases in equal measure. Historically, these professions were focused on real estate development and infrastructure engineering; today, we are seeing the development of professions focused on creating and managing services and operations. In 1898, Sir Ebenezer Howard published a seminal paper in London that started the garden-city movement (in response to the consequences of the Industrial Age) to provide citizens, especially factory workers, with healthier environments, and the first planned "garden city" of Letchworth (30 miles north of London) began construction. Also in 1898, the

United States began studying this early work from the UK and held its first urban planning conference in New York City, bringing together the disparate professions of architects, public health officials, and social workers.[64] In that era, urban planning education evolved from the interactions of civil engineering, architecture, medicine, public health, and sociology. Harvard created its first course in 1909 and offered its first degrees by 1923.[65] By the 1960s, urban planning included urban studies, becoming closely associated with the social sciences and economics as well. Today over 70 universities in the United States offer accredited graduate or undergraduate degrees in urban planning.[66]

Now the world's universities have begun leading much of the teaching and research efforts for this fourth era of cites, transforming urban planning and design into a new field called urban science, which includes urban informatics and technologies, uses geographic information systems labs, and focuses on urban modeling and simulation and such issues as urban mobility.[67] Urban science includes the new scientific ideas about cities as well as the growing amount of available real-time and historical data and computational methods to advance data-driven solutions. Cross-cutting topics range from urban design to civil engineering and from applied mathematics to statistics and public policy. The University of Warwick, Tokyo Metropolitan University, and Universidad Politécnica de Madrid offer degrees in urban science.[68] In the United States, examples include Northeastern University,[69] which initiated a master's degree program in Urban Informatics in 2014, and New York University's Center for Urban Science and Progress (CUSP),[70] which graduated its first cohort of Urban Science and Informatics Master's Degree students in 2014. These and other programs in U.S. universities expand on traditional urban planning and design curricula to include the relatively new field of urban informatics and incorporate both big picture concepts like data privacy and new technology infrastructure as well as real-world problems such as noise, buildings, transportation, resilience, and emergency response.

The Centre for Advanced Spatial Analysis (CASA) of University College London, started in 1995, is recognized as the first urban science university research institute.[71] A survey done in 2013 by Michael Batty, the initial Director of CASA, identified more than 40 centers worldwide and many more are conducting individual projects today with their local governments provided as paired partners. While the field of urban science research is young, present trends suggest that, by 2030, urban science institutes should connect thousands of researchers and represent more than $2.5 billion in annual R&D investment to advance sustainable, resilient, and smart urbanization and transfer that knowledge to the public sector.[72] The SENSEable City Lab at MIT, started in 2004, is recognized as the first university urban science laboratory in the United States.[73] The Urban Scaling Working Group at the Santa Fe Institute, which started in 2005, and the Urban Center for Computation and Data, a joint effort of the University of Chicago and Argonne National Laboratory, started in 2012, are also leading research here in the United States.[74]

2.4.1. Urban Science Tools for Interactive City Modeling

Early interactive modeling tools are already being used to create data-driven, interactive, tangible, 3D urban observatories and urban decision-support systems (DSS) designed to engage non-expert stakeholders for city development along green, convenient, and connected dimensions.

One example is the CityScope project developed by the City Science Initiative at MIT Media Lab.[75] CityScope combines physical scale models (made of LEGO bricks) and 3D projections of urban digital data to form a hybrid physical-virtual reality platform that enables multiple stakeholders to engage in urban decision-making. In observation mode, the CityScope visualizes urban data sets, real-time traffic flows, and social media as well as simulated data such as energy consumption or solar access, so that users can toggle between information layers. In active mode, the CityScope allows users to physically move elements of the platform (such as buildings or roads) to simulate alternative urban outcomes. For example, if a user moves buildings onto an empty site, then the CityScope will visualize the corresponding increase in the population density and the effects on traffic, energy use, and the demand on city services. Working with the city of Boston and the Barr Foundation, the Media Lab customized the CityScope to address the problems, and experiment with an array of solution tradeoffs, to greatly improve transportation access in the historically disadvantaged Dudley Square district in Roxbury, Massachusetts (see Appendix E).

2.4.2. Practitioner Certification and Accreditation Programs

The Green Business Certification Institute (GBCI) offers credentials for practitioners who are versed in creating green buildings. It was established in January 2008, with the support of the U.S. Green Building Council to provide independent oversight of the LEED project certification and professional credentialing processes. The LEED Professional credential exams are recognized by the American National Standards Institute, the (private) U.S. standards-setting coordination and oversight body.[76] Today, 180,000 practitioners have LEED credentials at various levels, which are required to be renewed by exam every two years.[77]

Practitioners are going beyond single buildings to create equitable, resilient, and sustainable districts and neighborhoods, but they lack an accreditation process. For the past four years, EcoDistricts.org has provided a training incubator, working with project teams from 37 cities to review and advance local projects and teach the intensive skills needed to regenerate urban districts. It is creating a new accreditation and certification process for green district projects (planned for launch in the spring of 2016). EcoDistricts accreditation will be a professional credential to build a network of protocol-trained practitioners. Their protocol will be the first of its kind to promote holistically district-level equity, climate protection, and resilience in urban redesign.[78]

The methods of recognizing education achievements are evolving to include new paradigms, as with the efforts in a number of cities to create digital badging of achievements by practitioners or students in a myriad of programs and opportunities that will be recognizable to future employers.[79] Also, in the spirit of citizen science, schools and municipal programs are asking residents to address urban challenges through the use of data and systems that are becoming accessible to ordinary citizens, thanks to open data and the Web.

2.5. Current Federal Government Initiatives

Federal agencies, including the Department of Commerce (DOC), Department of Transportation (DOT), Department of Energy (DOE), and some early coordinated programs also involving the Department of Housing and Urban Development (HUD) and the Environmental Protection Agency (EPA), are implementing nascent technology-based programs for cities. The White House Smart Cities Initiative of September 2015 also announced the private, non-profit MetroLab Network, which pairs city governments with local university research labs using Federal R&D funding to foster research relevant to specific city problems. Some of the sample activities are listed in the table below and further described in Appendix C.

Table of Federal Government Initiatives

Agency	Initiative
Department of Commerce	• Smart Cities – Smart Growth Business Development Mission to China[80] • Digital Economy program • NIST – Global City Teams Challenge[81] • EDA – Strong Cities, Strong Communities Economic Visioning Challenge[82]
	• EDA – Regional Innovation Strategies Program[83] • Census – CitySDK (Software Development Kit) [84]
Department of Transportation	• Smart City Challenge[85] • Ladders of Opportunity Initiative[86] • Transportation Investment Generating Economic Recovery (TIGER) grants[87] • Transportation Infrastructure Finance Investment Act (TIFIA) loans[88] • Partnership for Sustainable Communities[89]
Department of Housing and Urban Development	• Connect Home[90] • Sustainable Communities Initiative Resource Library[91] • National Disaster Resilience Competition[92] • Renew 300 (along with DOE and EPA) [93] • Promise Zones Initiative94,95 • Public housing programs[96] • Partnership for Sustainable Communities
Department of Energy	• Better Buildings Solution Center[97] • Cities Leading through Energy Analysis and Planning (Cities-LEAP) [98]
Environmental Protection Agency	• Partnership for Sustainable Communities • Water Infrastructure Finance and Innovation Act (WIFIA) financing[99] • Water Infrastructure and Resiliency Finance Center[100] • Brownfields Program (grants and technical assistance)[101]
White House in conjunction with other Federal agencies	• Place-based policy framework
	• Smart Cities Initiative[102] • US Ignite[103] • MetroLab Network (MLN) • Networking and Information Technology Research and Development Program (NITRD),[104] including Smart and Connected Communities framework[105]

3. A National Platform for Sharing Information, Software, Results, and Best Practices

Many cities across the world are implementing examples of innovative problem solving. Drivers are using apps that work with city-provided road closure data to navigate city streets more efficiently. Emergency (911)-dispatch centers are integrated with third-party smart-phone apps to help Good Samaritans know when, where, and how someone nearby needs CPR. Electricity, water, and natural gas meters are connected to the cloud to give subscribers fine-grained control over their resource usage. As discussed earlier, cities are using sensors and real-time data to solve specific problems in areas such as health, transportation, sanitation, public safety, economic development, sustainability, street maintenance, and resilience. Cities and communities can now use technology tools for much finer-grained access and management of their streets, above-ground assets, below-ground assets, land, and building. These early successes reflect the early stages of the fourth transformation of modern cities. But there is an uneven implementation and distribution of solutions across cities, highlighting a need for more effective approaches to data integration and sharing. The causes and consequences of this unevenness are summarized in the following table.

Causes		Results
• Lack of universally accepted platforms and standards • City incentives drive a focus on local issues, sometimes to the exclusion of more widespread concerns • Incomplete awareness of available applicable solutions • Unknown ROIs • Procurement is lengthy and not designed for iterative, agile technology-based solutions • Inability to support larger communities of users outside of the city	➡	• Idiosyncratic implementation • Uneven distribution of solutions • Expensive implementation • Smaller cities are disadvantaged • Rarely produce software usable by other cities

Though some de facto conventions are appearing through open data and other efforts, there are few private and no public mechanisms today to distribute the new knowledge and data associated with innovations comprehensively across the nation's cities. There is no "app store" specific to city applications, though the equivalent/such functionality is emerging in commercial cloud services (e.g., Socrata's Open Data Portal[106] platform or Amazon's State and Local Government marketplace[107]), proprietary enterprise, and Internet-ofThings applications. Over time we anticipate that the civic innovator community will build systems that work across and between multiple cities to deliver insights and capabilities unavailable today. A comprehensive information infrastructure for cities to use and share does not exist today and is needed to make significant progress.

3.1. City Web

An information-sharing platform would help to extend these innovative activities beyond their local confines, benefiting all cities, including those that lack the capacity to innovate on their own. PCAST sees both the potential and the beginnings of such a platform and refers to it here as "City Web." Following the pattern seen in other industries and sectors, existing systems available on the Internet can be used to create the app stores, marketplaces, online media, communities, and data and analytics products specific to city districts (and cities overall). Making the most of specific city-innovation experiences, the City Web would be a place for cities and their partners to make available descriptions and non-proprietary elements of solutions that have been implemented, tested, reviewed, rated, and used by other cities, thereby reducing the time and complexity needed for today's procurement cycles. Beginnings can be seen in the sharing of best practices broadly through the National League of Cities,[108] for specific kinds of innovation (e.g., the Department of Transportation's Research Data Exchange,[109] or for specific cities-focused communities of practice, such as foundation grantees pursuing common goals).[110]

The goal of the City Web is to allow the accumulation and replication of urban solutions and associated data and technologies in ways that benefit cities with different sizes, different technological know how, and different financial capabilities.

Technical requirements placed on cities and their staffs will only increase over the coming years. Large, high-capacity cities such as Los Angeles, New York, and Chicago understand this trend, but they, too, face multiple demands with limited resources. The City Web would ameliorate these demands in the same way that mobile apps and app stores are allowing non-technical individuals to benefit from the capabilities provided by today's powerful software and hardware. Mobile apps distributed by app stores make huge numbers of solutions widely available, transparently reviewed, and easily updateable.

The following table highlights some of the needs the City Web might address.

Table of City Web Opportunities

	Today	**Tomorrow**	**Future**
Goals	*Solve local issues.*	*Solve local issues and support future iterations and interoperability by moving to the cloud and app stores.*	*Solve local and general issues, support future iterations and interoperability, increase available options, and decrease entry costs through marketplaces.*
Information sharing between cities	Vendors, consultants, social networks, nongovernmental organizations, and conferences	Wiki and online community	Ratings, recommendations, reputation, etc.
Community-based software development	Limited; most implementations are proprietary and closed-source	Online repositories to facilitate open source code	Community management
Software applications **Data distribution systems** **GIS repositories** **Visualization** **Data analytics**	Individually procured bespoke, closed systems, proprietary systems, and/or locally-hosted servers	Software as a Service (cloud) and app stores (local)	Online marketplaces

The City Web builds upon and extends five areas of emerging activity:

1. A growing set of technology-savvy stakeholders that includes businesses, residents, civic organizations, and researchers;
2. New practices and standards for data creation, data annotation, metadata attributes, data searching, data sharing, and data privacy;

3. Technical protocols and application program interfaces (APIs);
4. Data analytics to manage and optimize city services; and
5. Integrated modeling and scenario evaluation to support policy and planning.

The City Web, like the Internet and the World Wide Web, would facilitate innovation from the bottom up; would be neither built nor operated monolithically; and would have no central authority to control innovation.[111] Taking a successful innovation in one city and applying it widely in other cities requires the development of standards (for interoperability and replicability) and the distribution of assumptions, knowledge, tactics, and data. These innovations must go beyond the predominantly proprietary Smart Cities platforms of today that are used by local governments to operate their services. The City Web also embodies the concept of a broader scope than today's platforms, analogous to the open data movement in recent years in that the applications and capabilities would be created by, and open for use by, many stakeholders. Such an open platform will enable not only the local government and industry, but also businesses and civic organizations to create new applications, optimize their development projects, create sophisticated computational models, and gain new insights.

This diverse set of stakeholders, ranging from citizens to non-profit organizations, and from businesses to local government agencies, is also creating data. Another advantage of the City Web is that it provides a powerful platform to anonymously combine the data collected from multiple cities and collected from multiple urban stakeholders. Running algorithms across a large set of this combined data can provide insights far beyond what can be seen from looking only at the data collected by individual stakeholders.

The evolution of City Web is shown in the figure below and outlined in detail in Appendix A.

The City Web will provide the platform that captures the results and facilitates experiments in other UDDs, often in other cities, to take advantage of the collective, accumulating breadth of knowledge. The two concepts are explicitly intertwined: Sharing information from the innovation ecosystem within UDDs can accelerate the evolution of the City Web, which then becomes a resource enabling better work within UDDs, which further improve the knowledge repositories in the City Web.

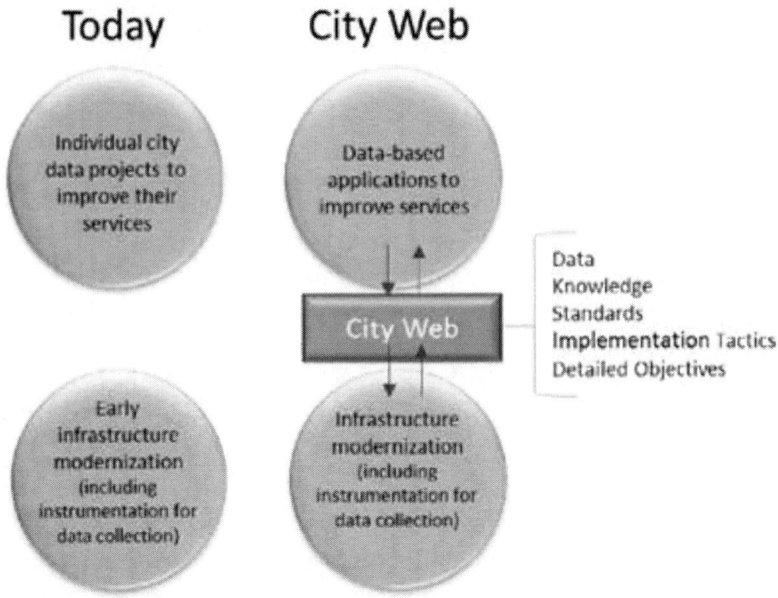

Figure. Transformation to City Web Platform.

The City Web provides an ideal repository for the large-scale networks (such as transit, waste-water management, electric grids, etc.) and the services (such as police, fire, etc.) used in these technology implementations. It could serve as a complementary data platform with high-resolution information at multiple levels (precursors can already be seen in cities like Chicago, New York, and Los Angeles). The accumulation and analysis of data would create a virtuous "learning loop" between the City Web and the results of the UDD implementations and experiments.

PCAST recognizes that cities are extremely diverse environments. Even with the ability to use knowledge developed by numerous cities, different places will want to follow different paths and make distinct choices. The City Web can help cities to adapt lessons and best practices to local conditions.

3.2. International Collaboration and Participation in the Development of International Standards to Help Create a Worldwide Industry

Standards are a common vehicle for propagating and benchmarking best practice, as well as for achieving interoperability. Helping to validate the idea that different kinds of technology are becoming increasingly important to the operation of cities is the emergence of international standards through the International Organization for Standardization (ISO), familiar to technology vendors and others for its quality-management framework[112] and suites of standards for specific kinds of interoperability. During 2014-2015, ISO introduced a standard aimed at helping cities around the world gauge and improve sustainability (part of the green dimension discussed in this report), ISO 37120: 2014, as a part of a suite of standards and part of an effort to promote benchmarking and learning among cities.[113] An international organization, ISO both builds on and informs local technology development and use activities; compliance with its standards (and other international standards) is key to participating in the increasingly global marketplace.

Specific kinds of technologies relevant to urban innovation are associated with specific sets of standards. For example, connected and autonomous vehicles (CAVs) are the subject of an evolving set of standards. Both the Society of Automotive Engineers (SAE International)[114] and, within DOT, the National Highway Traffic Safety Administration (NHTSA) have developed standard systems for evaluating vehicular autonomy.[115] The interoperability associated with CitySDK service development kits for cities originated in Europe in 2012;[116] as noted above the Census Bureau launched a U.S. version, and Github provides international availability for these resources.

Computing-related standards will be an important component of the City Web. But standards will also play an important role in the diversity of other products that will contribute to technology-enabled cities.

4. Opportunities for the Federal Government to Accelerate Progress

The Introduction to this report explains how cities are changing, both at home and abroad. Section 2 summarizes some of the ways in which present and future advances in technology promise to improve the infrastructure that supports and enhances city life. It provides a partial summary of the many projects going on both in the United States and elsewhere to design, deploy, and experiment with technology for one or more aspects of city infrastructure. In light of all the ongoing activity, why should the Federal Government increase its participation beyond the Federal programs summarized in Section 2? Section 3 provides one answer—seizing the opportunity to share local and individual computing and information technologies for cities on a national scale. This Section elaborates on a number of other important reasons:

- Economic competitiveness. There will be significant markets and jobs associated with advances in cities. Other countries are becoming more active. The United States should seize this new, multi-trillion-dollar business opportunity, including technology exports.
- Creating new jobs to support expanded development and implementation of the technologies discussed in this report and the revitalization of specific districts and ultimately larger areas of cities.
- Extending the benefits to all city residents. Experimental research programs and private-sector investments often target younger and more affluent communities, in part because there are fewer complications, and in part because that is where the participants live. The Federal Government has both the responsibility and the opportunity to extend the benefits of technological advances to underserved city residents. Enhancing the quality of life for all city residents, in disadvantaged as well as more affluent areas, will help cities function better overall.
- Amplifying the results of investments the Federal Government already makes in cities. Many Government agencies, notably HUD, DOT, EPA, and DOE, fund aspects of city infrastructure. Investments in forward-looking improvements will pay off over many years.
- Improving infrastructure that is critical for homeland security and for resilience to climate change and disasters.

4.1. International Activities and U.S. Competitiveness

While several Federal agencies increased their efforts to implement technology-based programs for cities in 2015 (and previous years), the rest of the world is not standing still. National governments in the UK, Germany, China, India, Brazil, and Singapore have stepped up with considerable organization, funding, and other resources to become leaders and aim their companies at what is now recognized as a multi-trillion-dollar worldwide opportunity. Anticipating another 1.1 billion people moving into Asian cities in the next 20 years, the Asian Development Bank is allocating $18 billion a year in grants and loans to help transform cities. Efforts in other countries are generating showcase innovations; they are also improving the quality of life for some of the poorest people.[117]

As an example of other commitments, in China, the government has made eco-cities part of its newest five-year plan.[118] In the Persian Gulf, entire new cities such as Masdar (United Arab Emirates) and Energy City, Qatar are being built with explicit sustainability goals.[119] In the UK, the future of cities has been an ongoing major focus by the counterpart to PCAST, the Council for Science and Technology, since 2013, and the United Kingdom has now appointed a Minister of Cities.[120] Appendix D summarizes a sample list of International programs under way.

And despite progress in many cities in recent years, U.S. cities continue to lag European and Asian cities with respect to walking and biking access.[121] The most walkable[122] cities in the United States hover around 8-11% modal share for walking (Seattle, Philadelphia, New York, San Francisco, Washington, D.C.) with Boston leading at 14%. In comparison, cities like Paris (61%), Madrid (36%), and Berlin (29%) not only lead but also continue to improve their walkability.[123] In biking, despite recent adoption and rapid growth of bike share programs and installation of bike infrastructure, the modal share of bike community averages hover around 1-2% for most cities. Portland leads the country at 6%, whereas Copenhagen is at 36% and has set a goal to exceed 50% by the end of 2015.[124]

Despite the city and Federal efforts described in Section 2, in almost every area of innovation, from clean energy to walkability, cities in the United States are behind when it comes to urban innovation. They run the risk of falling further behind those in other countries and regions of the world where national governments are investing in the transformation of their cities, including the creation of new ministry positions and agencies dedicated to cities. The re-platforming of cities around the world is a race the United States cannot afford to lose, as it generates demand for new products, new companies, and new skilled jobs in the effort to produce the best environments to attract International residents and companies.

4.2. What Should the U.S. Government Do?

Introducing into cities those technological infrastructure advances that are economically robust, inclusive, effective, and achievable is a complicated process. It requires the integration of many technologies and stakeholders, demonstration projects in city districts, coordinated interagency and public-private R&D investment, an information-sharing platform that would help to extend these innovative activities beyond their local confines and benefit all cities, standards setting, workforce development, international cooperation, and significant public/private investment. As shown in the following figure and elaborated in the sections that follow, the Federal Government has an essential role to play.

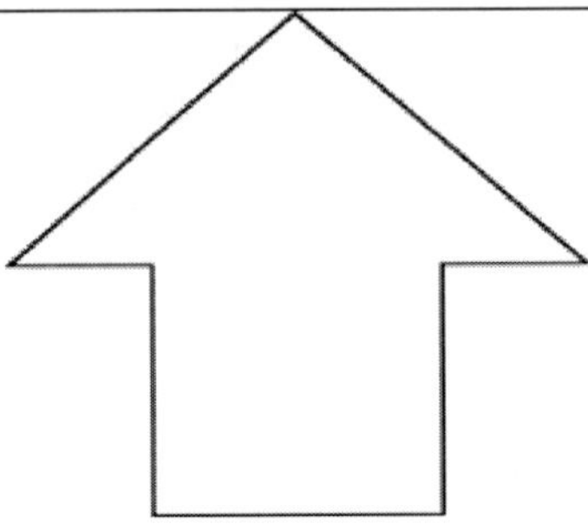	**Today** • Near-term Local Technology Introduction • Transformations Happening in Urban Development Districts • City-based Pilot Projects • Profession of Urban Science • Current Federal Government Initiatives
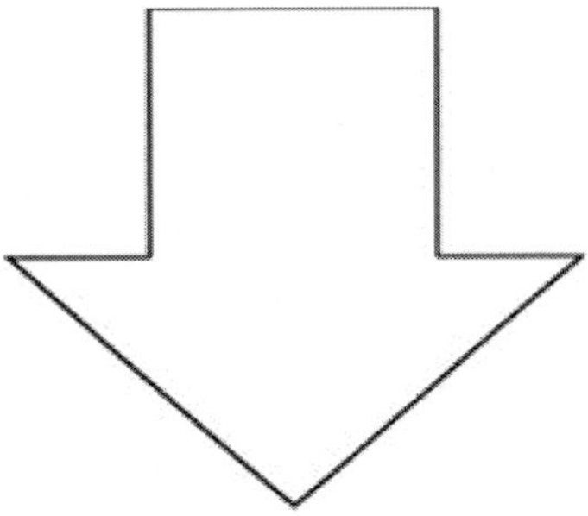	**What's Missing** • Multi-agency Public/Private Programs for City and District Technology Adoption • Integrated Demonstration Projects • Education and Training of Future Workforce • Platform for City-to-City Collaboration • Funding for City and District Innovation • Coordinated R&D Across Government Agencies

Figure. Opportunity Landscape.

4.3. Coordinated Interagency Programs and Incentives for City and District Technology Adoption

The fragmentation of Federal activities that help cities and/or foster innovation diminishes the potential for transformational change. An integrated approach to supporting new technologies that can improve the lives of people in cities—engaging multiple Federal agencies as well as State and city entities and the private sector— would pay enormous dividends.

Doing so would expand upon recent efforts to coordinate Federal support for individual cities. At the same time, a better integrated Federal effort to encourage technological innovation in cities would enhance ongoing Federal programs that focus on economic disparities and physical infrastructure. A coordinated effort has the potential to address many of the reasons outlined at the beginning of this Section.

Given the many Federal agencies with missions and programs that relate to cities, and the many opportunities to leverage one another's work, enhanced mechanisms for coordination of Federal activity are needed. Given the potential for city-to-city sharing of knowledge and experience, coordination outside the Federal Government is also needed. The key to success in this new era where districts can pilot and nucleate change comes with an integrated approach of combining the use of multiple new technologies, streamlining the regulations around land use and zoning (a local responsibility), carrying along or evolving the existing infrastructure (e.g., street grids and conduits), and sharing resources when possible. No single Federal agency has all the tools to help local governments make the most of the opportunity. An integrated approach of all the stakeholders, including many agencies of the Federal government working together, can achieve much more than any one alone. This, of course, is one of the lessons of place-based policy.

Coordination will not happen by chance. Innovation will not come to most cities without incentives, encouragement, and assistance. To make progress in an effective way, PCAST recommends that a funded interagency initiative, the Cities Innovation Technology Investment Initiative (CITII), be established. As outlined below, its responsibilities, in addition to interagency coordination of government programs, would be to sponsor both city/district and government-located demonstration projects, to facilitate workforce education and training programs, and to initiate a process to create a shared software and data platform under the direction of a consortium composed of all stakeholders.

4.3.1. Demonstration Projects

The Federal Government cannot fund all the innovation projects that will move U.S. cities forward, nor should it. Competitive programs are very effective in motivating groups to create meaningful projects for change. For relatively little spending, many local multi-stakeholder teams are energized to come together to produce well thought-out proposals under very tight deadlines. The promise of funding motivates the testing of a complex integrated system that would be impossible to create otherwise. But even the runner-up teams, which have put plans in place, are motivated to find funding to implement their ideas. While the transformations in cities are largely happening bottom-up, coordination and acceleration of activity is something that the Federal Government is uniquely suited to help do. The Department of Transportation Smart Cities Challenge[125] was launched in December 2015 and is a promising forerunner to competitions that could be established for cities or districts.

The Federal Government can also benefit from its own in-house demonstration projects. Some agencies have natural districts such as campuses and military bases that could house innovative technology solutions to their infrastructure challenges.

4.3.2. Certification and Accreditation Programs to Create the Workforce of Tomorrow to Implement the New City Technologies

Making the most of new technologies in cities implies having a workforce with the necessary skills, not only within city governments but also within local communities. Training certificates, curriculum, and mini-degrees can help to create the workforce to implement technology-based innovation in their own communities and be certified to help others; creating a workforce (job creation) to lead this fourth era of cities. There are opportunities to build on the Administration's Ready to Work,[126] Tech Hire,[127] and other job-driven trainin g128 initiatives, a broadening base of activities aimed at improving the fit between local training local employment opportunities; agency (notably DOE) efforts to foster training associated with innovative technology relevant to cities; and new and evolving capabilities to use technology both to deliver training and facilitate the match of people to training and to jobs.[129] Technology suppliers, community colleges, and others should align in developing programs and associated credentials that will expand the workforce capable of deploying new technologies in cities. Existing government programs at all levels can help to target those programs in ways that help create jobs in disadvantaged urban communities.

4.3.3. Certification Standards and Goals Beyond the Building Level

Improving the quality of life in different ways at the district level would benefit from new district- and city-scale certifications that reward excellence in, for example, local energy management and other environmental outcomes. The objective of such certifications is to go beyond LEED-ND certification to create a rolling challenge for urban innovation as well as provide a means for setting specific targets and measuring progress. Such certifications should encourage innovative solutions for achieving the highest levels of performance, feature ways to combine function (e.g., energy-efficiency) with attention to equitable distribution of benefits (e.g., credit for use in disadvantaged areas), and plan for periodic revision of their parameters to ensure continued challenge and open-ended innovation.

With a well-recognized rating system, districts can more effectively identify and achieve high standards (for example for energy and/or water conservation or reductions in greenhouse gas emissions), with additional incentives through recognition by a public designation (e.g., "Energy Star Districts" or some other suitable term). A tiered recognition system would provide incentives for districts within cities to deploy energy-efficient technologies, distributed renewable power generation, healthy mobility (e.g., walkable neighborhoods, bike sharing, electric vehicles), micro-grids, and other known contributors to greenness, mobility, and socioeconomic enablement. Model neighborhoods that achieve, for example, carbon-neutrality and the highest levels of energy autonomy and resilience would be awarded "Platinum" status, earning attention and attracting businesses and residents.

4.3.4. The City Web

Section 3 and Appendix A describe a vision of a national shared computing infrastructure, the City Web, that would accelerate the goal of using technology for the benefit of all urban areas, be they large or small, rich or poor. By virtue of shared interfaces, tools, data, and standards, the City Web would enable adaptation to change, cost savings, and decision support across the United States. The Government is the natural convener to bring together the many stakeholders, public and private, that could make that vision a reality.

4.4. Recommendations

The President's Council of Advisors on Science and Technology (PCAST) calls for the Federal Government to take a more integrated approach to supporting new technologies that can improve the lives of people in cities. Doing so would expand upon recent efforts to coordinate Federal support for individual cities. At the same time, a better-integrated Federal effort to encourage technological innovation in cities would support ongoing Federal programs that focus on economic disparities and physical infrastructure. A coordinated effort has the potential to:

1. Help the United States seize a new, multi-trillion-dollar business opportunity, including technology exports;
2. Create new jobs to support expanded development and implementation of the technologies discussed in this report and the revitalization of specific districts and ultimately larger areas of cities;
3. Enhance the quality of life for all city residents, in disadvantaged as well as more affluent areas, helping cities function better overall; and
4. Improve infrastructure that is critical for homeland security and for resilience to climate change and disasters.

Given the many Federal agencies with missions and programs that relate to cities, and the many opportunities to leverage one another's work, enhanced mechanisms for coordination of Federal activity are needed.

RECOMMENDATION 1. The Secretary of Commerce, working with the Secretaries of Housing and Urban Development, Transportation, and Energy, should establish an interagency initiative, the Cities Innovation Technology Investment Initiative (CITII), which will encourage, coordinate, and support efforts to pioneer new models for technology-enhanced cities incorporating measurable goals for inclusion and equity.

CITII is intended to foster durable coordination among agencies that can or do support innovation relevant to cities. Accordingly, representation from the Departments of Commerce, Energy, Defense, Homeland Security, Housing and Urban Development, Transportation, Treasury, the Environmental Protection Agency, and the Army Corps of Engineers is essential. For connection to the research objectives discussed below, representation from the National Science Foundation is desirable; also desirable are representation from the Department of Agriculture, for attention to urban agriculture, and from the Department of Labor, for attention to job-driven training opportunities. The Smart City Challenge launched by the Department of Transportation (DOT) in 2015 models the envisioned combination of focus on innovation and competitive selection. PCAST's encouragement of innovation in districts is intended to support a broad array of innovative efforts deployed in a set of areas within a set of cities.

(1a) Under the leadership of the Department of Commerce, CITII should create and develop, by December 31, 2016, an initial blueprint for how U.S. agencies can foster systemic innovation across many dimensions of cities.

Although such agencies as the Department of Transportation and the Department of Housing and Urban Development have considerable emphasis on cities, the Department of Commerce, through the efforts of many of its components, has already taken some important steps to coordinate and lead in smart-cities activities, an important segment of the larger landscape of technology innovation for cities, positioning it well to lead in creating a long term plan before the end of the Administration.

(1b) In advance of developing that blueprint, CITII should, through the use of competitions following the model of the Department of Transportation's Smart Cities Challenge, undertake activities to accelerate adoption of new technology. It should fund five districts with funding in the range of $30-40 million each, from existing sources in its constituent agencies, with at least two of the districts in low-income communities.

(1c) CITII should work with Federal agencies that have campuses that could be Federal "districts of experimentation," such as the Department of Defense with military bases, to create living trial/test-bed and demonstration areas that can serve as model districts. These collaborations would recognize and encourage innovation in natural/self-defined districts composed of single-owner campuses owned and/or operated by the Federal Government.

(1d) CITII, working in concert with the Department of Housing and Urban Development and the Department of Labor, should design training programs, including certificate programs, that can connect urban technology innovation to jobs development.

(1e) Under the guidance of CITII, the National Institute of Standards and Technology (NIST) and the National Science Foundation (NSF) should initiate a convening process to establish the prospects and parameters for an independent, community-driven body to define, implement, and evolve the City Web (a City Web Consortium), similar to the World Wide Web Consortium (W3C)[130] and the Internet Engineering Task Force (IETF),[131] which emphasize standardization based on broad adoption of common and proven approaches. The Federal Networking and Information Technology Research and

Development (NITRD) program should work with CITII to coordinate existing activities to share data, models, and software tools among cities and stakeholders.

The new MetroLab Network of partnerships among cities and research Institutions, along with National Laboratories, could help facilitate the City Web Consortium. The City Web Consortium would work with private sector and research laboratory technologists and city Chief Technology Offiecers to develop and maintain the protocols of a decentralized cloud-based site (similar to the Internet) that brings together, via API access, the full range of shareable City Web assets, with an emphasis on the kinds of support for innovation addressed in this report along with existing technology-based innovations including government apps and Open Data source-code collections on GitHub,· the Peer Network at Code For America, SourceForge, and a variety of open or commercial forums around the theme of innovations in cities.

(1f) The U.S. Chief Data Scientist (CDS) should work with Federal agencies in CITII to identify types of data useful in the design and implementation of projects that improve public safety, public health, citizen mobility, and other desirable goals. The CDS should help the agencies promote new ways by which various stakeholders can develop and share best practices and data, attending to privacy and security. CITII should also develop a framework of incentives to motivate all stakeholders to share their data with others. This should include a common use-based model for ensuring privacy and ethical data use.

RECOMMENDATION 2. Because PCAST believes technology will play a crucial role in revitalizing low-income communities in cities across the United States, the Department of Housing and Urban Development (HUD) should embrace technological innovation as a key strategy for accomplishing its mission.

With its history in urban development, HUD should become an originator of new models for making cities more nimble and more adaptable to technological change. The Department will require the staff capacity and the funds on the scale necessary to support advances in urban technology and innovation. HUD should immediately appoint a Chief Technology Officer or Chief Innovation Officer. The Department should adjust future budget requests to establish programs such as innovation laboratories and other data and technology resources common to other agencies.

4.5. Federal Government Funding for Technology Adoption

Many early projects are being implemented in greenfield or depopulated brownfield districts. While costly, these projects can relatively easily integrate new technologies. In contrast, districts that are highly populated, with older, less efficient technologies not yet near the end of life, will face more challenges in introducing multiple technologies together. Even the prospect of lower long-term operating costs may not be enough to justify both significant capital expenses and disruption, even for the prospect of making their districts more livable. Federal Government funding or loans could be very helpful in meeting the capital needs while reducing disruption by accelerating the switchover to the new systems.

RECOMMENDATION 3. The Administration should seek legislation enabling two financing programs that will support cities and municipalities to develop Urban Development Districts (UDDs) and to introduce significant new technology in their communities.

(3a) The Administration should continue to seek approval by Congress of an innovative new Qualified Public Infrastructure Bonds (QPIBs), which, as originally proposed by the Administration in January 2015, would, if approved by Congress, provide an incentive for more private investment in technology-based innovation in cities. QPIBs extend benefits of municipal bonds to public-private partnerships.

Although the proposed ATII program will help early innovators, additional debt financing will be needed to support more extensive innovation. Some of the borrowers will be public-private partnerships, either by design or due to the integration of public and private ownership of existing infrastructure systems. Because tax-exempt financing is available only for wholly publicly owned infrastructures, QPIBs, proposed in the Fiscal Year 2016 and 2017 budgets and requiring authorizing legislation, would make tax-exempt financing available to public private partnerships.

(3b) The Department of the Treasury should create an Advanced Technology Infrastructure Incubator (ATII) Program. ATII would facilitate loan funding of technology-based innovation in Urban

Development Districts at levels that allow for meaningful change and impact, particularly in low-income districts. This would be scored, based on risk, by the Office of Management and Budget at an appropriate small fraction of the value loaned.

ATII is intended to overcome two impediments to implementing new technologies in cities: (1) the difficulty of making large-scale capital investment (e.g., for new energy or water infrastructures) by public agencies and private companies that need to allocate existing resources for operating and maintaining legacy infrastructure systems—accelerating infrastructure renewal is hard to finance; and (2) the difficulty of achieving integrated infrastructure development in a current context dominated by siloed control and fragmented ownership. Eligible borrowers would include State and local governments, public agencies, public-private partnerships, and private companies. Loans would be repaid by rates or fees assessed on projects. It is expected that the integration and upgrade of these systems will result in cost savings that will allow for the repayment of debt on legacy systems.

A larger, scalable, model of funding requires legislative authorization. Acknowledging that hurdle but also contemplating the future, the ATII would expand the CITII program by offering loan funding to all CITII-competition finalists rather than the few winners supportable through discretionary agency budget funding. The program would require an initial appropriation of $10 billion, which would allow for the financing of at least $100 billion of infrastructure-retooling projects. It would makes loans to State, municipal, private, and non-profit entities that are implementing local demonstrations aimed at creating livable and connected districts and that are using the City Web. Loans would include features that are unavailable or costly in the private capital markets and that provide incentives for borrowers to pursue ambitious infrastructure innovation. First, the program would allow borrowers to delay draws on the loan for up to five years at no cost, enabling them to match financing with their construction cycle. Second, borrowers would not be required to pay interest for the first five years of the loan, and they would be permitted to capitalize interest for up to five years thereafter. This would allow projects time before they are required to generate cash flow to repay the loan. Loans would be offered for up to 30 years at Treasury rates, and up to 50 years at Treasury rates plus a small term premium that will help reduce the cost of the loan to the Federal Government.

4.6. Formalized Coordination of R&D across Government Agencies

Although 2015 began to see an emphasis on R&D funding for cities, more attention needs to be paid to the interactions and issues that cut across agencies, to promote complementarity and synergy, and more interdisciplinary R&D. While efforts have already begun to foster coordination under the NSTC Subcommittee on Networking and Information Technology R&D (NITRD)[132] and NSF, the kinds of R&D expected to be key include computation, data, sensor platforms, and integration technologies, in particular, for transportation (especially motor vehicles and transit), energy (building and industry energy use, plus electricity acquisition, generation, and distribution), water, and other city-infrastructure services. Given earlier discussions regarding the interplay between technology and norms of behavior, it will also be essential to integrate social, behavioral, and economic sciences with these more traditional infrastructure sciences.

Coordination should start with an inventory of research projects across all agencies. Since the goal is to engage science and technology to improve the lives of people living in cities, it will be crucial to further develop research on the empirically based understanding of the linkages between social and economic human behavior, urban infrastructure and services, and other aspects of urban environments. Such research must be leveraged and further developed with the objective of identifying new technology-enabled solutions for urban problems and for assessing proposed solutions. There also needs to be a more formalized mechanism to propose technology-enabled grand challenges for cities and city districts.

Every day cities face operational challenges and resource constraints that focus attention on what might be done now. By contrast, research with a much longer-term horizon is required to be competitive in replatforming our cities. Consequently, the emphasis should be on balancing and, indeed, integrating both the development of better tools based on current understanding of urban systems (short-term, engineering) and the pursuit of deeper understanding of the fundamental workings of cities as complex systems (long-term, fundamental research).

RECOMMENDATION 4. The National Science and Technology Council (NSTC) should create the Urban Science Technology Initiative (USTI) Subcommittee to coordinate Federally funded research and development (R&D). Building on more limited coordination efforts such as those revolving around smart cities, USTI would connect different kinds of infrastructural and other physical technology R&D with data- and ICT-oriented R&D. USTI should begin its work by creating an inventory of relevant R&D projects and grant programs across all agencies. PCAST also recommends that the research work of USTI be informed by the implementation work of CITII, and vice versa, a process likely to be in place in the beginning through the participation of the same agencies in both interagency activities.

APPENDIX A. THE CITY WEB

An information-sharing and collaborative development platform would help to extend these innovative activities beyond their local confines, benefiting all cities. With the growing momentum of open data, increasing innovation leveraging the Internet and relatively new technologies such as cloud and software-as-a-service, and partnerships between cities, universities, and National Laboratories we see both the potential and the beginnings of such a platform and call it "City Web." Following the pattern seen in other industries and sectors, existing systems available on the Internet can be used to create the app stores, marketplaces, online media, communities, and data and analytics products specific to city districts (and cities overall). Following specific city innovation experiences, the City Web would be a place for cities and their partners to make available descriptions and non-proprietary elements of solutions that have been implemented, tested, reviewed, rated, and used by other cities, thereby reducing the time and complexity needed for today's procurement cycles. It should be the primary repository for publishing and sharing the data and implementations that result from work that is directly supported by government funding.

The goal of the City Web is to facilitate and accelerate the accumulation and replication of urban solutions and associated data and technologies in ways that benefit cities with different sizes, different technological now how, and different financial capabilities.

It is natural to point out that, as with daily life today, the technical requirements placed on cities and their staffs will only increase over the coming years. Large, high-capacity cities such as Los Angeles, New York, and Chicago understand this trend, but they, too, face multiple demands with limited resources. The City Web would ameliorate technology-adoption challenges in the same way that software-as-a-service, mobile apps and app stores are allowing non-technical individuals to benefit from the capabilities provided by today's powerful software and hardware. Mobile apps distributed by app stores and software capabilities customized and provided as online services make huge numbers of solutions widely available, transparently reviewed, and easily updateable.

Table of City Web Opportunities

	Today	**Tomorrow**	**Future**
Goals	*Solve local issues.*	*Solve local issues and support future iterations and interoperability by moving to the cloud and app stores.*	*Solve local and general issues, support future iterations and interoperability, increase available options, and decrease entry costs through marketplaces.*
Information sharing between cities	Vendors, consultants, social networks, nongovernmental organizations, and conferences	Wiki and online community	Ratings, recommendations, reputation, etc.
Community-based software development	Limited; most implementations are proprietary and closed-source	Online repositories to facilitate open source code	Community management
Software applications **Data distribution systems** **GIS repositories** **Visualization** **Data analytics**	Individually procured bespoke, closed systems, proprietary systems, and/or locally-hosted servers	Software as a Service (cloud) and app stores (local)	Online marketplaces

The City Web concept builds upon and extends five areas of emerging activity:

1. A growing set of technology-savvy stakeholders that includes businesses, residents, civic organizations, and researchers;
2. New practices and standards for data creation, data annotation, metadata attributes, data searching, data sharing, and data privacy;
3. Technical protocols and application program interfaces (APIs);
4. Data analytics to manage and optimize city services; and
5. Integrated modeling and scenario evaluation to support policy and planning.

The City Web would facilitate innovation from the bottom up, being neither built nor operated monolithically and with no central authority directing or regulating innovation. Taking a successful innovation in one city and applying it widely in other cities requires capturing and documenting key specifications and proving value and interoperability in the field, leading to the development of standards (for interoperability and replicability) and the distribution of assumptions, knowledge, tactics, and data. An open approach emphasizing replication and interoperability will also be essential to moving beyond the often fragmented and proprietary Smart Cities platforms of today that are used by local governments to operate their services. Indeed, the City Web aims for a broader scope than today's platforms by being open for use by many stakeholders, beyond the local government, such as businesses and civic organizations to create new applications, optimize their development projects, create sophisticated computational models, and gain new insights.

Urban Development Districts (UDDs), as outlined in the body of this report, provide the physical space for experiments and innovations that grow understanding about how technology and innovation affect the urban landscape, including information and people flows, changes in the physical infrastructure, goods/vehicles movement, energy use, and other types of flows. UDDs provide a small enough real urban environment to conduct in-depth experiments that provide tangible results. The City Web will be the platform that captures those results and facilitates experiments in other UDDs, often in other cities, to take advantage of the collective, accumulating breadth of knowledge. The two concepts are explicitly intertwined: Sharing information from the innovation ecosystem within UDDs can accelerate the evolution of the City Web, which then becomes a resource enabling better work within UDDs, which further in turn improves the knowledge repositories in the City Web.

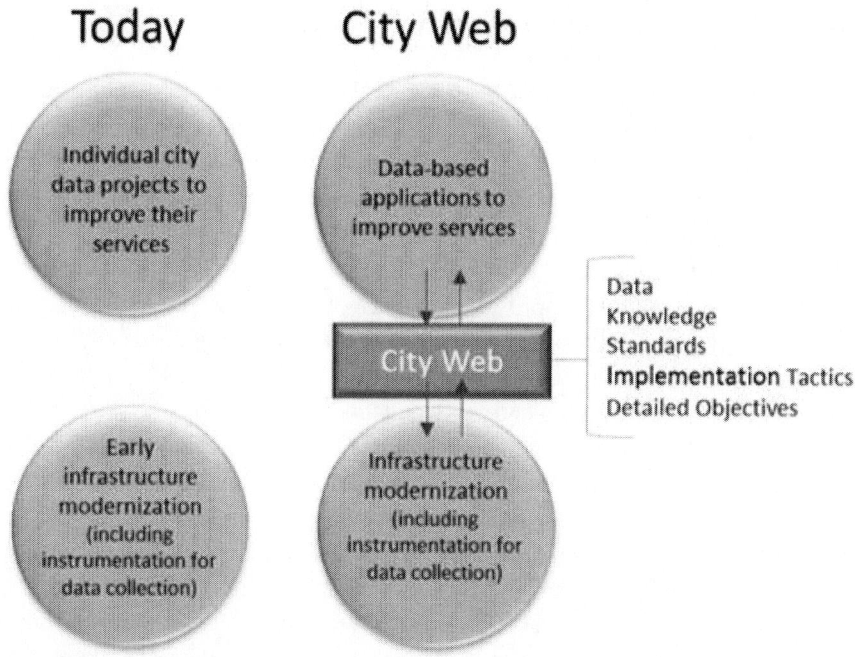

Figure. Transformation to City Web Platform.

The City Web provides an ideal repository for the large-scale networks (like transit, waste water management, electric grids, etc.) and the services (like police, fire, etc.) used in these technology implementations. It could serve as a complementary data platform with high-resolution information at multiple levels. The accumulation and analysis of data would create a virtuous "learning loop" between the City Web and the results of the UDD implementations and experiments.

PCAST recognizes that cities are extremely diverse environments. Even with the ability to use knowledge developed by numerous cities, different places will need to follow different paths involving distinct choices. The strategy of using the City Web and the experimentation performed in Urban Development Districts to capture the details of implementation and measurement of impact and results will be essential in facilitating adaptation of best practices to local conditions. Below we detail each of the five key areas of emerging technology and activity that will be central to building the City Web.

A Growing Set of Technology Savvy Stakeholders

The most important function of a City Web is to create a platform for urban innovations to help solve difficult and persistent urban problems. While we discuss in this section many issues directly related to technology, data, and optimization, the most important results of any initiative to improve cities are improvements to the general quality of life, inclusion, and opportunity of urban residents. Thus, the use of technology in cities must ultimately be judged by how much it improves the lives of people as social, civic, and economic agents. A platform can help to make such improvements easier through lowering the barrier of entry for cities in their efforts to deliver and manage services using online and mobile technologies.

A differentiator today is the growing set of technology-savvy urban stakeholders, from citizens to non-profit organizations, and from businesses to local government agencies. Problem-driven collaborations between very different entities are always difficult. Our expectation is that a successful City Web, supported by public policy at multiple levels, would provide a powerful new platform to align diverse interests, coordinate action, and promote agreement on solutions. A platform accessible to a wide range of stakeholders makes possible greater transparency and with it better coordination and solutions that are simpler to test, validate, and improve upon.

Recent developments point to an interesting and powerful convergence between individuals and organizations with new technological skills and the problems of cities, articulated as a new bottom-up civic technology movement focused on user-centric design solutions. Civic-minded organizations, such as "Code for America,[133] have developed new models of collaboration, based on volunteers and individuals with know-how from academia and industry who regularly collaborate with city service providers and in some cases choose to be stationed in cities for extended periods of time. Companies such as IBM, Cisco, McKinsey, and Siemens have also led the way developing the concepts, technologies, and services toward making cities "smarter," highlighting many of the important possibilities, especially from an engineering or management perspective. These efforts are not only bringing technology to urban problems, they are also bringing new problems to technology, making it possible to create new services and economic value from the point of view of entrepreneurs and businesses.

Civic non-profits are also increasingly using technology and data to make their point, in ways that can often supersede the ability of local governments or businesses to collect and interpret data and that can forge new collaborations between government and civil society. An example is Data Driven Detroit, [134] an organization that has compiled and organized much information about the city of Detroit, including its land use, vacant property, environmental quality, patterns of employment and other important indicators of quality of life in a struggling urban area. Such civic-minded organizations can augment the capacity of cities to compile and understand their data, while creating networks of collaboration between many stakeholders. They can also contribute to the education and training of communities in new technologies and quantitative analysis on issues of direct relevance to their lives.

Explicit collaborations between city governments and universities or National Laboratories are also exploring many of these possibilities, bringing diverse aspects of research and development closer to local governments and to local residents. The nascent MetroLab Network[135] is a good example of this kind of city-university partnerships. Originating in Pittsburgh with Carnegie Mellon University and an initial set of like-minded city-university pairs in Boston, Chicago, New York City, Portland, Seattle, and South Bend, its partnership concept and expansion to over 20 cities to date was supported by the White House Office of Science and Technology Policy. Initial areas of the Network's focus are public-private partnerships on infrastructure and services, as well as issues of democratic governance, public policy, and public management.

There are enormous benefits in coordinating the creation of knowledge with local action in all these ways. First, used well, data and technology can allow a quicker convergence to facts and results between organizations with different agendas, thus facilitating a truly democratic, transparent, and effective political process. Second, the use of technologies proposed here can also foster convergence between government, the private sector and scientific organizations by facilitating the evaluation and testing of proposed solutions. Finally, the possibility of the convergence between science, policy, technology, and entrepreneurship creates a new space for new advanced STEM education and training, connected to practical local problems with enormous economic scope for applications elsewhere.

New Practices of Data Creation and Open Data Portals

A clear trend is the increasing amount of data made public by city governments. These data are already facilitating new insights and solutions for local governments, businesses, and technology developers and promise to play an essential role in understanding and planning cities in the future.

An essential ingredient in the use of these new data is the development of the ability for cities to set measurable objectives and acquire information that allows them to assess their progress. New digital services are enabled by both advances in technology and by the open data-sharing culture that has been catalyzed by recent Federal Open Government and Open Data[136] initiatives. As a result, a growing number of city and local governments are publishing much of their data in more standardized (machine-readable) formats. That activity may be linked to broader progress in how cities use ICT: A key aspect of agile service development is working in the open and allowing interested stakeholders and the public to watch, learn, and participate in this work. The U.S. Digital Services Playbook includes 13 "plays" or resources to aid strong digital service delivery, including a section titled "Default to Open."[137] A discussion of the methods and benefits of agile and inclusive development in government can be found online.[138] The U.S. Office of Management and Budget TechFAR resources can be also be found online at GitHub.[139]

Nevertheless, of the nearly 20,000 incorporated cities and over 3,000 counties in the United States, only a very small fraction currently shares data or has created open data portals. There is a long way to go before local governments are able and willing to digitize, use, and share data universally. The struggle of the 1990s and early 2000s was to move from paper processes to digital applications; individual information solutions were typically developed for particular departments or applications; and many cities have yet to make this transition. Where cities moved to digital processes one department and function at a time, they have been left with an accumulation of non-integrated solutions and fragmented data.

Progress would be helped by broadly adopted and implemented data organization and exchange protocols as well as for a greater effort in improving the quality and completeness of published data. This is easier said than done: The recent availability of standard open data portal products, such as Socrata's cloud-based platform, has enabled many cities to rapidly publish hundreds of data sets.[140] Although many dozens of open data applications have been developed, only a subset have proven useful, much less transformative, for transparency, cost reduction, or improved operations.

The number of cities opening data has grown quickly over the past 5 years, with now on the order of a hundred[141] cities and places operating open data portals. The trend is clearly seen in larger cities or places with more resources. The use and publication of data require a level of capabilities, from implementing the movement from paper to digital processes, to archiving, curation and analysis (e.g., for sensitive issues). A quick glance at those in the box, City Open Data Portals, shows that many smaller places are starting to participate in the movement towards open data.[142]

Even cities with large IT budgets share this struggle to generate and use data internally. This is the result of a variety of factors: What data are collected during city operations? Are they annotated and standardized so that they can be shared meaningfully with third parties, and what privacy policies and regulations govern their use?

Where cities have transitioned toward machine-readable data, many of the data sources cannot be published fully, or in some cases at all, due to privacy or other kinds of sensitivity of the data. For example, for privacy reasons, identifying information must be removed from 911 and 311 call records prior to publication, and while the GPS-tracked locations of snowplows can be published, the same information about police vehicles cannot.

City Open Data Portals

Many cities are making much of their data publicly available in open data portals. This includes improving data quality and completeness and publishing it according to standards that make it easily usable for analysis and the development of applications by businesses and civically minded organizations. Below is an example view of a crowd-sourced Website created by Code for America, the Sunlight Foundation, and the Open Knowledge Foundation to begin to catalog and categorize open data portals.

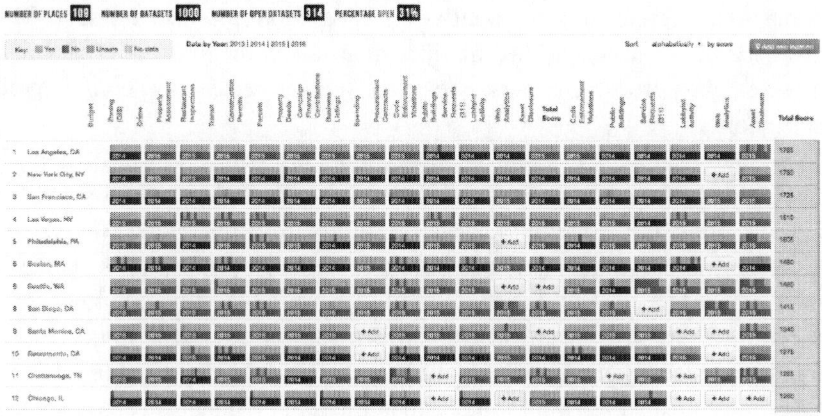

While privacy is centrally important, if cities are to support human development and equitable opportunity it is essential to understand how cities are actually working for particular individuals and locations. Meanwhile, because data derived directly or indirectly from human activities are increasingly common, there are large amounts of data inside of cities that touch upon all aspects of daily life. Examples include:

- Data generated by city governments and utilities on the supply and demand of urban services (energy, water, public transportation, zoning, public spaces);
- Dynamic maps of the urban fabric, ranging from those derived from frequent and high resolution remote sensing (sub-meter) and derived classifications of land use to existing maps from private technology companies, the movement of city and public vehicles, and crowd-sourcing efforts and methods, such as OpenStreetMap[143] and Photogrammetry;[144]
- Environmental quality data from sensors, individuals, and private company analysis (local weather, including insolation, wind and temperature, which are affected by the urban built environment; pollution, noise, disorder); and
- Social and economic data, such as 911 and 311 call data, small-area statistics from U.S. Census and other surveys, public real-estate transactions, crime maps, and local quality-of-life indices.

In these and other cases, information that would be valuable to improved city operation and efficiency is often unavailable due to regulatory restrictions or due to the legal and competitive considerations of data holders. Many universities have access to health, education, or corrections data for analysis for research purposes, where the data are protected by confidentiality agreements.

Similarly, universities and national laboratories have powerful modeling tools and access to data about city buildings, demographics, employment, and transportation—but not utility usage or utility reliability data. In isolation, these data sources yield some insight into issues such as the interdependencies between access to transportation and opportunities for employment or education. Combined, such data could provide guidance for more effective programs aimed at energy costs, allowing for investment in addressing root causes (e.g., insulating walls) rather than ongoing symptoms (e.g., assistance with heating bills).

Exploration of new agreements and arrangements for enabling such analysis, and the benefits to utilities, residents, and cities alike, will be critical. Potential solutions range from establishing or designating trusted third parties that combine data for analysis to developing algorithms that support privacy-preserving analysis. Both functions are already served today, with Federal Government support, by National Laboratories and research centers at universities.

One of the fundamental functions of the City Web will be not only to capture and promote new technology and approaches to data curation, description, and exchange, but also to facilitate such exchanges between data stewards—cities, utilities, companies, service providers, agencies—and trusted third-party analysis services provided by National Laboratories and universities.

Technology and Data Exchange with Standardized Protocols and Application Program Interfaces (APLs)

New models to share data over the Internet across different systems and to create ecosystems of interoperable and coordinated applications and technologies allow for novel possibilities for the development of a City Web. Through these technologies the City Web can be adapted to the needs of a particular city and simultaneously generate building blocks and standards easily customized and adapted to other places, possibly in collaboration with businesses, researchers, and civically minded developers.

Traditionally, an IT department of any organization—including a local government—would develop discrete applications and associated databases. As database and application technology evolved, packages of associated applications and databases enabled departments to share related data, such as payroll, personnel, and recruiting functions. Cloud computing and "software as a service" allowed many organizations to outsource their data centers, subscribing to application and database services rather than operating them locally. These developments have been revolutionary, yet it remains the case that enterprises consist of many departments, each running systems of integrated applications and databases.

Although this fragmentation is both technically and organizationally challenging, the concepts of APIs and standard data-exchange protocols and formats (e.g., XML, JSON, CSV), have been key to the success of cities in effectively utilizing data from across their organization. Standard data-exchange protocols are essential to pulling data from their native sources into an integrated, distributed system that can support analysis, applications, and publishing, such as through a Web portal. APIs define functions that can be built into applications to access and use data in these standard formats.

APIs and other Web resources allow any organization to share their data online in some chosen standard format. Applications in turn can become very modular, so that "mash-ups" that integrate different functions (often stand-alone applications that can be interconnected) and data can be easily developed, combined, and further refined.

This means that a vital property of a City Web is, like the Internet itself, to develop, curate and promote useful APIs, utilizing widespread data exchange protocols, so that new data and applications (and associated underlying business processes) developed in or for a particular city can be easily shared and further developed by others and so on. In so doing, the City Web aims at supporting the conditions for fast improvement in IT technologies for all cities, without the need for top-down coordination, e.g., via meetings or other slow, traditional methods.

A good illustration of the power of APIs and standard data exchange, combined with data-description standards, is the Open311 Ecosystem. The 311 system is a dedicated call service for reporting non-emergency issues in cities, such as noise complaints, potholes, or street-light outages. As noted on the Open311 Website, the system "first began with an API for Washington D.C.'s 311 system, but it really become a community when the leadership of San Francisco and the support of organizations like OpenPlans, Code for America, and even the White House brought many cities, companies, and organizations together into a productive collaboration."[145] The key to this ecosystem lies in the combined power of data description standards (encoding types of 311 calls consistently across cities), data-exchange protocols (formatting data to be machine-interpreted), and APIs (specific functions allowing any application developer to write a 311 application, such as reporting by mobile phone rather than voice call).

In the United States, Open311 has become the standard way to develop this urban service in many different cities and encourage innovation from many technology developers without creating lock-in or dependence on a single provider, as is required when the data and applications are bundled without external APIs. The system is now adopted internationally, including in cities such as Toronto, Lisbon, and, via World Bank initiatives, in developing nations such as Mozambique, Tanzania, and the Philippines. In this way a complex service, initiated in large cities, is becoming easily available and usable even in small cities[146] and in developing nations.

Application Programming Interfaces (APIs)

APIs are specifications that define how data and commands are passed between application programs. Examples of successful APIs include those used by the many types of Web browsers which communicate through well-defined APIs to the many types of Web servers to deliver and display websites over the Internet. While there are many types of browsers and many types of Web servers, the APIs are documented and adhered to in order to allow virtually any browser on any device to work with any type of Web server.

A second illustration is in transport and mobility. The General Transit Feed Specification (GTFS), developed by a Google-led technical community as a common format for public transportation schedules along with geographic data, has similarly enabled independent parties to develop applications that allow users to compare time and cost of routes, check schedules and locations for public transit, etc. There are now dozens of transit APIs being used.[147] For instance, Transit App[148] has created a smart-phone application that integrates public transit data and APIs with those of new car sharing services (e.g., Uber, car2go, auto-mobile, and others) and bike-share services,[149] easily creating entirely new possibilities for more sustainable mobility in cities around the world. These types of data and services is typically integrated with mapping services, e.g., via the Google Maps,[150] Bing,[151] or OpenStreetMap's[152] APIs and with digital satellite images, from Digital Globe,[153] NASA, or USGS.[154]

In the energy sector, the Department of Energy's (DOE) National Renewable Energy Laboratory[155] has developed an API that provides solar energy generation information for hypothetical rooftop solar systems and can be easily integrated with weather APIs for estimating real time performance for these systems and with real estate information, e.g., from Zillow,[156] Trulia,[157] or Walk Score.[158]

Data-exchange standards and APIs are critical to progress for an increasingly important source of new urban data, the Internet of Things. Buildings, for example, are moving toward digitally integrated control systems, where traditionally the disparate systems such as HVAC, elevators, doors, and lighting have been independent, non-interoperable, and without APIs for external application development or data exchange.

Ultimately, the danger of viewing cities as collections of independent, vertically integrated systems (buildings, transportation, utilities, etc.) is that innovation at the intersection of sectors, where often the most promising solutions lie, is crippled by the discontinuities between these separate systems. This is true even if within each vertical there are open standards for (internal) interoperability.

An important goal of the City Web, then, is to bring a broader context and a new technological substrate to these activities, promoting the creation of systems that are not only open and interoperable within buildings, or between vehicles, but between independently developed sector solutions. By reducing the bespoke nature of these traditionally vertically integrated sectors, the City Web can promote and facilitate new approaches, technologies, and solutions at critical intersections.

Data Analytics for Prediction and Optimization

Cities are taking increasing advantage of bigger data and the use of advances in applied mathematics and computer science (algorithms) to analyze that data to inform operations and other decisions. Common examples are efforts at optimization through the statistical prediction of certain types of events or conditions and the identification of statistical anomalies as events to be understood and/or acted upon. The most powerful of these predictions rely on not only open data but sensitive, internal data. For instance, police departments in Los Angeles and other cities in California and in Chicago have used predictive analytics to identify urban areas that are statistically more likely to experience violent crime during a given day (crime hot spots).[159]

Similarly, one of the common operations across most local governments is the need to perform inspections, such as for fire, elevator, or food safety. New Orleans and New York City are developing predictive algorithms to identify probable fire hot-spots and guide fire-safety inspections, while Chicago is using similar techniques to predict rodent infestation and food safety. In these cases, algorithms provide a statistical likelihood of the given safety issue and can thus be used to preferentially schedule inspections based on expected risk (see box on Data-Analysis to Improve Food Safety), which may provide improvements versus random inspections.

Data-Analysis to Improve Food Safety

With new sources of data from city processes, social media, and urban sensors it has become feasible to begin to identify leading indicators for common conditions or types of events and developing algorithms for statistical forecast, and quantifying the uncertainties behind these forecasts. One example, below, is the optimization of food safety inspections, statistically classifying food establishments with respect to probability of food safety violations. The graph shows that optimizing inspections based on risk improves the timeliness of finding food safety violations relative to the more traditional random inspection schedules, on average finding violations 7.4 days earlier in the inspection cycle. (Credit: City of Chicago Department of Innovation and Technology).

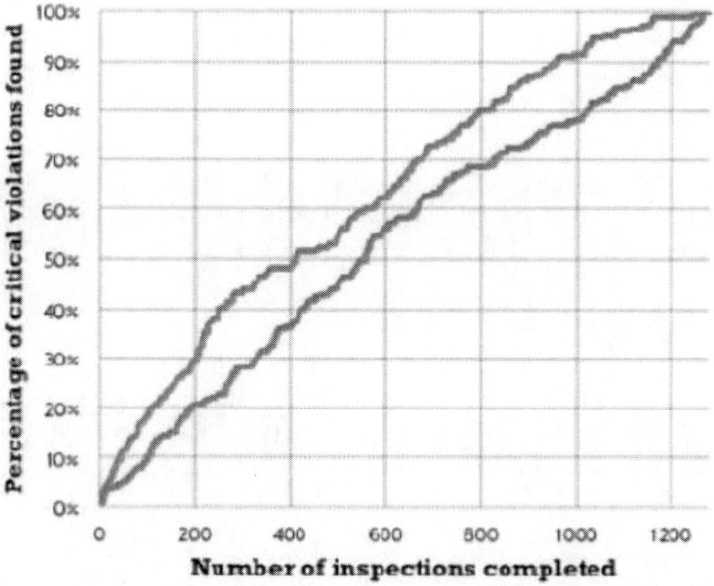

Each of these emerging applications involves common components: identification of leading indicators, data models, and algorithms to combine these into statistical predictions, and optimization algorithms to translate such predictions into inspection schedules. As these methods continue to improve it is expected that they can both save money and, more importantly, improve public safety.[160]

Making the most of such tools will involve their integration into summary tools; some have begun to emerge. Los Angeles developed a dashboard capability that is being adopted by dozens of cities (see box on The Mayor's Dashboard).[161] Chicago has packaged its data integration and analytics capabilities as open source, cloud-hosted systems that can be readily replicated without large IT staff or resources. Similar commercial products are offered by multiple vendors, as well as a wide variety of aggregators. A tool for making comparisons between cities is now being developed under ISO 37120.[162]

We expect to see these capabilities mature with further research, development, and experimentation.

The Mayor's Dashboard

The Mayor's Dashboard was originally created in the City of Los Angeles and is now being used by more than 20 different municipalities and two congressional offices. Developed using free open source software (FOSS) with an investment of $9 and five days of donated development efforts, the public Dashboard is hosted on Github.com and uses data syndicated through the city's open data portal. Replacing manually created reports printed on paper, the dashboard works with any device capable of displaying HTML5 and is easily customized for management, education, and other uses.

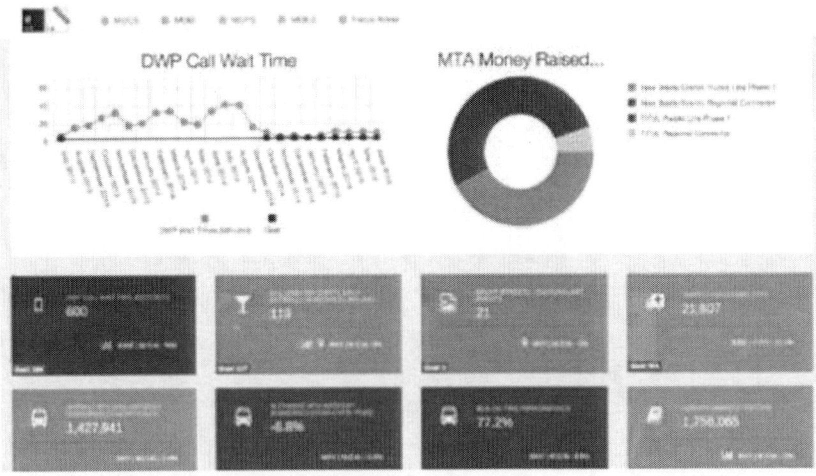

Such tools illustrate some of the integration that a City Web could provide, although the City Web would extend beyond city government, per se: The City Web would provide a platform on which civic and commercial entities can partner with local governments in using analytics to address issues by combining data from multiple sources.[163] Examples may involve the active management of city-service vehicle routes (using UberPool or Bridj algorithms) or applications to help individuals find space in homeless shelters (using AirBnB algorithms). Because their algorithms and data define their businesses, companies like Uber, Bridj, and AirBnB prefer to keep such assets proprietary. Current research supports capabilities for entities to use each others' data and algorithms without their being published. Such capabilities could be of particular benefit to cities, with a City Web providing the virtual meeting ground for access to data and analytical tools from private and public sources.

Integrated Modeling and Scenario Evaluation

Further opportunities to use emerging urban data and models also result from progress in visualization and from fast-increasing computational capabilities, which are being nurtured broadly through both the Federal Networking and Information Technology Research and Development program[164] under the National Science and Technology Council and the new (2015) National Strategic Computing Initiative,[165] which expands on DOE's Exascale Computing initiative.

Large-scale computational models have long been used in traffic simulation and other, relatively narrow, urban applications. The vision of a City Web is associated with the development of more complex, integrated models. Although integrated models of cities have a history going back a few decades, they have had only limited influence on urban science and policy because they are used even less than narrower, function-specific models.[166] The use of models that simulate an entire city in detail is constrained by their requirements for large amounts of computation, specialized expertise, and, depending on the application, tendency to run more slowly than in real time.

The greatest progress has related to the modeling of natural phenomena. For example, it is becoming possible to model wind and water flow and solar irradiation through the 3D urban built environment, creating the conditions to track the effects of weather and climate on physical aspects of cities and evaluate some important facets of their environmental quality and potential resilience to extreme natural events. Also, computational simulations and forecasts of energy demand and regional transportation systems are increasing in fidelity and becoming more useful and accurate at giving city managers and planners better situation awareness, extrapolation to future situations, and support in building scenarios that can better clarify policy choices. These models typically describe short-term scenarios (minutes to weeks) for particular cities; more effort is needed to make these tools more general. Detailed epidemic simulations and other agent-based models are also becoming more common, giving policy-makers a window on other aspects of how urban societies may respond to extreme events and health crises.

Better assimilation of data relating to current situations has begun to enhance the value of large-scale computational models, which remain limited in their capacity to address such important factors as individual human behavior and social dynamics. Models that are not refreshed by data quickly lose predictability over time, especially when changes of human behavior are important. Strategies for data assimilation in real time can mitigate these issues and create the conditions for large-scale urban simulation to be more useful and informative. How good these models can become remains a topic of research and development.

Integrated modeling has four main objectives:

1. The integration of various disparate data streams in ways that make explicit reference to space, time, and the physical city and many of its socioeconomic characteristics;
2. Closing the loop on urban management and policy by readily quantifying gaps between intended urban services and actual conditions and by identifying the emerging locations and impacts of congestion, pollution, noise, crime, and other urban challenges;
3. Providing the basis for simulation to inform longer-term urban planning and policy through scenario building and forecasts for comparing different policy options; and
4. Creating an environment to develop and test integrated urban theory and its implementation as policy and to discuss and evaluate the tradeoffs of the adoption of new technologies.

Integrated modeling of urban areas that can exploit new urban data sources and integrate design and engineering models, tested at smaller scales, is on the horizon. It may build on models developed at different scales, from the district to the metropolitan area, that are integrated together as needed.

Partnerships between universities, National Laboratories, and cities can develop these capabilities, providing interfaces that are tuned to specific end-users (operations managers, policy makers, etc.) for particular uses and analyses of the data and information.

The City Web can help to transform urban modeling from an arcane or proprietary set of tools limited to narrow sets of specialists into the kind of broad tool that is visible and usable by anybody to better understand a city, though there may also be advanced modules to enable science and policy and facilitate entrepreneurship. A City Web with interoperable open data formats, APIs, and modular components can support a large ecology of developers and users, including private corporations and open-source developers. Such an ecosystem should be conducive to many forms of technological and organization innovation and the use of the increasing variety of information about urban environments to create new value as a source of human development and economic growth.

Conclusion: City Web and the Vision of an Information-Enabled City

The City Web expands beyond individual city efforts on open data, engaging such efforts through open data formats and open APIs and coalescing as a platform to creatively use new information technologies to solve urban issues, through wide collaborations among all sectors of society and many cities. In this fashion, the ecosystem of urban information innovations can leverage what has happened with the Internet to support innovation and the creation, adaptation, and evolution of a wide variety of urban analyses, insights, and value-added services. Cities are systems of systems, characterized by complex interactions between different sectors, such as transport and energy. The City Web creates new opportunities for higher-level integration and potential optimization across urban networks (such as mass transit and bike-share programs). It would naturally offer high-level support for goals such as sustainability, resiliency, accessibility, equity, transparency, security, and, of course, efficiency.

To realize the City Web there must be research, development, and demonstration that go beyond today's open or sharable data, APIs, and early successes in predictive analytics. For example, partnerships between cities and research institutions have potential not only to innovate and demonstrate such new capabilities but also to use research institutions as trusted third parties where data can be combined and analyzed under rigorous controls.

PCAST believes that the City Web is a timely concept for several reasons. First, there is tremendous innovation that has resulted from open data initiatives. Tools and platforms are being developed that are beginning to expand from early adopter cities as the value of data-savvy city operations and policy becomes more apparent. To capitalize on this momentum, the City Web must enable new data-sharing capabilities that allow these initiatives to penetrate key areas of urban life, whether related to energy, health or socioeconomic equity related to transportation, safety, education, and general access to a decent life and opportunity.

Second, across every important urban infrastructure sector—transportation, buildings, communications, energy, water—advances in technology are creating new service models and associated opportunities for integration of infrastructure elements through data exchange. The City Web would provide opportunities for these currently independent advances to create solutions that exploit the many common technologies, methods, and approaches between sectors and to enable innovation across sectors through open interfaces and data standards.

The City Web will be built by many of the same institutions, companies and individuals that have previously created the Internet, the World Wide Web, and the open data movement. Today the opportunity is for the civic organizations, businesses, universities, and National Laboratories to apply similar principles and approaches and many of the same technologies to work with local governments to create the City Web.

APPENDIX B. DATA-ENABLED PILOT PROJECTS

Improving Public Health and Asthma with Data-Driven Services

Respiratory conditions and asthma, in particular, are the focus of present efforts from many cities across the Nation. Data collected by the Centers for Disease Control (CDC) at the national level indicates that asthma affects about one in 12 adults, especially the elderly, and nearly one in 10 children.[167] It also accounts for more than $56 billion in annual costs, 14.2 million physician office visits and 439,000 in-patient discharges. Statistically there is a higher incidence of asthma in larger cities, with Los Angeles and Philadelphia topping the list.[168] Demographic studies also show that the incidence of asthma is statistically associated with socioeconomic challenges, especially poverty and low-quality housing.[169,170]

Traditional studies do not get to the heart of the problem. Asthma is generally associated with factors that are very local, for example, mold or pests inside the home or heavy traffic or proximity to industrial facilities outside. A number of cities are developing strategies based on new technologies and data that allow them to track the challenges experienced by patients and identify more proximate causes of this common health challenge.

The diversity of approaches[171] and their potential integration in terms of a systemic new approach to combat asthma form a particularly compelling case for the initiatives advocated in this report.

For example, Pittsburgh is exploring a program called Breathe Cam with panoramic cameras that provide near real-time views of Pittsburgh. Citizens can use the Breathe Cam online to zoom-in on sources of emissions, use computer vision to quantify the amount of pollution emitted, make recordings of pollution events, and scroll back and forward in time to compare visibility and identify systematic polluters.

Detroit, Los Angeles, Lowell (Massachusetts),[172] Boston, and New York City[173,174] are using hospital-admissions data to retroactively identify areas of the city with the highest incidence of asthma.[175] And Louisville, Kentucky, in collaboration with IBM Smart Cities and Propeller Health, is providing residents with a free GPS sensor and phone app for their inhalers.[176]

The city of Chicago is working with the Argonne National Laboratory and the University of Chicago, with funding from the National Science Foundation to deploy the Array of Things—a city-wide network of 500 lamppost-mounted sensors with an important air quality component.[177] This initiative has some parallels to the network of sensors developed by LinkNYC and Sidewalk Labs in New York City, using retrofitted sites of old public phones for new purposes,[178] including sensors in collaboration with Argonne National Laboratory and providing Wi-Fi at thousands of locations in the City.

The city of Chicago is also analyzing its non-emergency complaint-call data to identify environmental issues connected to the incidence of asthma, such as pestilential infestations. Data scientists identified more than 30 leading indicators predicting rat infestation by analyzing 12 years of 311-call data ranging from calls about rat infestation to graffiti and flooding, as well as data from weather services and social networks. Maps generated by predictive analytics enable inspections and treatment that are significantly less skewed by frequency bias, the observation that more wealthy residents are more likely to use 311 than those in distressed neighborhoods.[179] The analyses allow rodent-abatement teams to look forward seven days, predicting where infestations will likely happen and helping the city of Chicago to get out ahead of them.[180]

Reducing Air Pollution with Shared Energy Use Data and Emissions Accounting

Containing and addressing global challenges like air pollution and greenhouse-gas emissions are most effectively done locally, in cities, as stressed recently by former New York City Mayor, Michael Bloomberg.[181]

In practice, this process requires that cities are able to account (quantitatively) for all their energy use and emissions. The tally must be precise enough that progress towards reducing emissions can be assessed on an ongoing basis. Although a number of U.S. cities have undergone such accounting exercises,[182] international standards are only now emerging that allow for comparative progress between places and over time. At present, it remains a daunting task for most cities to account for all their local energy use and related emissions and use these data in ways that help guide strategic analysis, policy, and future quantitative assessments.

Although some basic tools have been developed associated with the emerging Global Protocol for Community-Scale Greenhouse Gas Emission Inventories (GPC),[183] developed under the recent agreement known as the *Compact of Mayors,*[184] these are fairly basic[185] and require further development. To compound these issues, cities that do not control their utilities struggle with even the most basic problem of obtaining data on energy consumption and transmission. A similar problem occurs around transportation and other fuels used in heating, which are difficult to account for in terms of consumption over space and time. But general quantitative procedures and an information infrastructure, data protocols, and analysis tools for localizing energy use and emissions quantitatively at the district level can help all cities collectively achieve these goals. Sharing real-time detailed data with cities can also offer immediate application and success.

Eliminating Deaths and Serious Injuries on the City's Streets Using Data-Driven Approaches

The economic success of cities is tightly tied to transportation systems. While railroads, airlines, and shipping systems have reached a high degree of safety, automotive transportation systems within cities remain a leading cause of death and serious injury for pedestrians, bicyclists, passengers, and drivers.

Data and analysis offer cities means to reduce the dangers of automobile-based transportation systems. Often referred to as "Vision Zero", the idea can be summed up as, "when a child runs after a bouncing ball into a residential street and a speeding car strikes and kills him, the Vision Zero philosophy maintains [that] the death shouldn't be seen as an unavoidable tragedy but as the result of an error of road design or behavioral reinforcement, or both."[186] Data-based analysis can reduce the number of opportunities for human error and other types of failures resulting in death or serious injury.

Vision Zero is being implemented using data analytics across a number of departments in San Francisco, New York City, and Los Angeles, among others. In Los Angeles, data were collected to create a visualization of the High Injury Network for use by all stakeholders,[187] such as families concerned about how to get their children to school.[188] An effort named the "Safe Routes to School" started in 2012 with the city's Department of Transportation developing a prioritization methodology using disparate data on collision rates, the number of children living within walking and bicycling distance of each school, and equity and health indicators to identify schools with highest need. The Top 50 schools are located on or near the city's High Injury Network, a network that comprises six percent of the streets and which accounts for 65 percent of pedestrian fatal and severe injury collisions. Data useful to decision-makers, whether municipal planners or individual drivers and pedestrians, are being distributed through websites and third-party mobile apps. These recent technical enablers are now allowing for greater work on the root causes of serious injuries and fatalities along multiple lines.

Improving Fire Prevention with Artificial Intelligence

New York City has roughly one million buildings. The New York Fire Department (NYFD) started using data mining and predictive analytics to determine which ones are most likely to erupt in a major fire. Roughly 60 different factors have been built into an algorithm that assigns each of the inspectable buildings with a risk score. The risk score now determines the order of inspection, as opposed to a process that returns to previously inspected buildings randomly or based on safety priorities. Fire prevention is particularly important to high-poverty neighborhoods with vacant or unguarded buildings that are most susceptible to fires.[189] The computer system under development at NYFD called Firecast. FireCast 3.0 will examine 7,500 factors across 17 city agency data streams and use artificial intelligence to track trends city-wide. For example, trash violations can now be correlated with fire threat levels. The FDNY now has an analytics unit and data scientists.[190]

Making Street Services Technology Efficient

The city of Los Angeles is currently in the process of adding Global Positioning Systems, sensors, and cameras to their street sweepers. This will allow the city to open streets for parking more quickly, track water usage, tune or change routes to real time priorities, and track coverage to make sure street sweeping is complete. Computer vision may facilitate reporting cracks in pavement, broken sidewalks, missing paint, missing signage, and using street sweeping as the continuous eyes for prioritizing infrastructure improvement.[191]

Crime Prediction

The University of Chicago's Harris School of Public Policy is working with Argonne National Laboratory and the Urban Center for Computation and Data to explore algorithms using eight years of crime-event data and current and forecasted weather to predict the probability of violent crime for each Census block across the City of Chicago and for each hour within a 72- hour horizon.[192] The key objective to this work, as well as to commercial systems such as recently announced by Hitachi,[193] is to enable police departments to deploy patrols more effectively based on better knowledge about "hot spots" with greater probability of crime during a given shift. Similar work was recently published by the Harvard University Center for the Environment[194] using 13 years of Chicago crime data to link environmental pollution and crime.

Improving Recycling by Integrating Public and Private Data in Real Time

The city of Los Angeles is rolling out a franchise-management system to integrate private waste companies into the cities' system of service calls, data tracking, and billing to work together to deliver yard waste services to multi-unit dwellings and commercial locations. This will double recycling efforts by allowing the city to expand tracking of waste and recycling beyond single-family homes, integrate private and public data systems, lower the need for more landfill, and use the collected data for infestation tracking.

This effort is similar to those taken in a variety of cities to spur the use of recycling and to divert materials from increasingly expensive landfills.

Crime Prediction

Using machine learning algorithms and eight years of Chicago crime data, the University of Chicago is developing a general-purpose tool for predicting crime probability on a census tract resolution based on place-based history and weather forecasts.

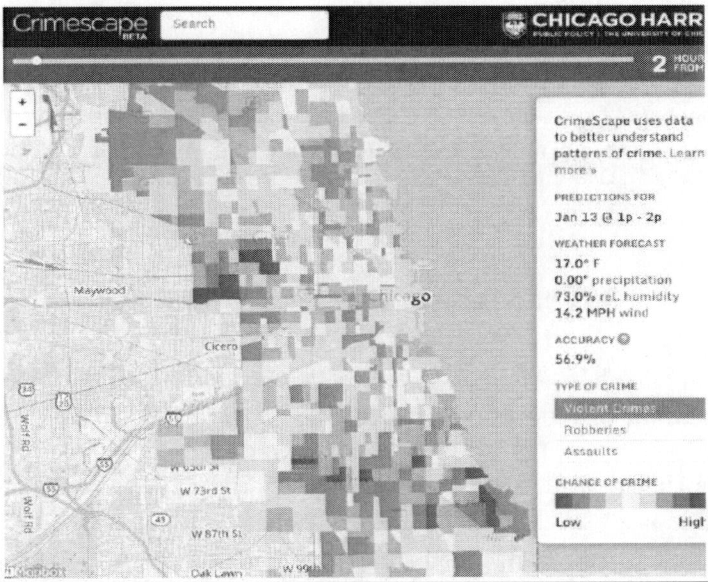

Load-Balancing of Street Systems through Crowd-Sourcing and Marketplaces

A number of apps have been published that let drivers and passengers identify shortest routes over city streets. Cities are sharing real-time data with these apps, and receiving reports from them, in an effort to optimize the use and management of city streets. Waze is a social media wayfinding app used by more than 1.5 million people in Los Angeles that consumes road closure, safety, and other data from the city and, in turn, provides to the City all of the crowd-sourced user reports of collisions, obstructions, and hazards every two minutes. These data are then integrated into the 311, contract administration (road construction permits), public safety, and emergency management systems as early alerts for potential service calls and reports of violations.

These systems are being extended into mobility marketplaces to include multiple transportation modalities. CitySight in Denver and Los Angeles has been built by Xerox that includes real-time availability and pricing from public transportation, ride sharing (e.g., Lyft and Uber), taxi, bicycle share, walking, parking, and private vehicles. This marketplace presents users with all available options prioritized according to the user's requirements of lowest transit time, lowest price, or lowest ecological impact. The marketplaces will be available on the Web, in apps, and on kiosks at physical transit points such as the airports, train stations, and public transit interchanges.

These apps rely upon real-time location services provided by the user's smart-phone or from automatic vehicle location systems installed on the buses and other vehicles from which data is distributed through the cloud or private networks.

Appendix C. Selected Federal Government Initiatives

Department of Commerce Initiatives

The United States Secretaries of Commerce (Penny Pritzker) and Energy (Ernest Moniz) led a Smart Cities–Smart Growth Business Development Mission to China in April 2015. It promoted U.S. exports to China by supporting U.S. companies in launching or increasing their business in the marketplace for Smart Cities–Smart Growth products and services.[195]

The Department of Commerce (DOC) has been focusing on the role of data as a factor that unifies its disparate components, and in 2015 it launched a Digital Economy program, both developments that increase its capacity to contribute to efforts to use technology to improve cities. DOC has been actively involved in cities through such components as the National Institute of Standards and Technologies (NIST), Economic Development Administration (EDA), and the Bureau of the Census, in addition to more targeted engagement via the National Oceanographic and Atmospheric Administration (NOAA), National Telecommunications and Information Administration (NTIA), and International Trade Administration (ITA). NTIA, for example, supports growth in broadband capacity across cities and other communities.[196] Overall, DOC has a lot of distributed technology capacity to partner with other agencies.

NIST: As an evolution of the Cyber Physical Systems effort under the aegis of the interagency Networking and Information Technology Research and Development (NITRD) program, NIST launched the Smart America Challenge in 2013 with the aid of Presidential Innovation Fellows and then the Global City Teams Challenge (GCTC) in September 2014 "to establish and demonstrate replicable, scalable, and sustainable models for incubation and deployment of interoperable, standard-based Internet of Things solutions and demonstrate their measurable benefits in Smart Communities/Cities."[197] The program's goal is to help communities improve efficiency and lower costs by learning from each other's experiments. The first round primarily promoted collaboration and started the process of developing international standards. It involved 64 teams of more than 50 cities and 230 global organizations. The results were demonstrated in an expo in June 2015, attended by 1,400 people. Following on its success, GCTC launched a second round of proposal requests in September 2015 and a kickoff workshop in November 2015, with a commitment of $5 million in FY 2016,[198] that will culminate in deployments in June 2017. The teams are international in scope and NIST has partnered with NSF, ITA, the Department of Transportation, States, and various trade associations, private sector corporations, universities, and non-profits. NIST's work on Cyber Physical Systems and the Internet of Things[199] connects it to both industry and the research community, as well as to other parts of the Federal Government.

EDA: The Economic Development Administration (EDA), which supports infrastructure improvements and related development in distressed communities,[200] is leading the Strong Cities, Strong Communities Economic Visioning Challenge featuring a multi-phase competition to award funding and expertise to projects that could best create targeted economic development in cities. Greensboro, North Carolina; Hartford, Connecticut; and Las Vegas, Nevada generated a combined 143 proposals and were chosen to run their own competitions in the second phase. Eighteen proposals received a total of $2.5 million and were announced in August 2015, which included 3 winners (a center for universities, firms, and communities to coordinate educational and business goals in Greensboro, a health care and medical technology cluster in Hartford, and an Unmanned Aerial & Robotics Resource Center in Las Vegas).[201] EDA further announced another $10 million in grants for FY 2016 for cities solving pressing issues in innovation and resilience.[202] EDA supports innovation and capacity-building through such vehicles as i6 Challenge grants to help start-ups, Seed Fund Support for geographically clustered "firms, workers, and industries that do business with each other and have common needs for talent, technology, and infrastructure,"[203] and Science and Research Park Development Grants.[204] Through such programs EDA contributes to Federal support for the Smart Cities initiative.

Census: The Census Bureau rolled out CitySDK (Software Development Kit) in June 2015, a project developed by White House Presidential Innovation Fellows to provide an efficient and easy way for public organizations to access and use Census data. That day, they also launched the open data challenge, a contest to get public and private company organizations to use the data in most interesting ways. Five finalists using open Census data were showcased on August 13, 2015 to show other Federal agencies ways to work with Census data. For example, a finalist in Minneapolis combined mobility, housing, hospital, safety, and community data to allow people with disabilities to find the best places to live and travel in Minnesota.[205]

Department of Transportation Initiatives

The Department of Transportation (DOT) has recently funded support for future experiments in parts of New York City and Tampa for connected vehicles. In December 2015, the Department of Transportation launched the Smart City Challenge to solicit proposals in 2016 and select, through a nationwide competition, a medium-sized city to receive $40 million in funding to implement "bold, data-driven ideas to improve lives by making transportation safer, easier, and more reliable" and particularly with support infrastructure for Intelligent Transportation Systems (ITS) and Electric Vehicles (EVs) and integrating in new norms of behavior.[206] It is expected that the other finalist proposals will be publically highlighted and likely to benefit, as a result, from engaging the private sector.

DOT has traditionally been an instrumental participant in connecting city residents to economic opportunity, and also creating transportation industry jobs, through their Ladders of Opportunity initiative[207] and Transportation

Investment Generating Economic Recovery (TIGER) grants that are awarded to fund capital investments in surface transportation infrastructure.[208] Since 2009, TIGER has provided nearly $4.6 billion to 381 projects in coordination with the Department of Housing and Urban Development.[209]

Department of Housing and Urban Development Joint Agency Initiatives

In July 2015, the Department of Housing and urban Development (HUD) and the White House launched Connect Home, a pilot program in 27 cities to offer over 275,000 low-income households access to Internet service at home, funded by the private sector.[210]

In March 2015, HUD announced that it had created a Sustainable Communities Initiative Resource Library to house the products of HUD's Sustainable Community Initiative existing 143 community grantees. This new online library became a repository for dozens of local and regional comprehensive plans, model codes, tools, and reports so all communities can learn from the successes of these innovators. The library serves as a showcase for the range of activities that grantee cities, counties and regions have taken since the first grant was awarded in 2010.[211]

In June 2015, HUD launched the second and final phase of the National Disaster Resilience Competition for finalists to compete for almost $1 billion in funding for disaster recovery and long-term community resilience. In the previous year, $181 million was set aside for communities in New York and New Jersey.[212]

In July 2015, HUD, DOE, and the Environmental Protection Agency (EPA) announced Renew 300 with a goal to target 300 MW of renewables, primarily community and shared solar installations, for low-and-moderate income housing by 2020. Federally assisted housing includes HUD's rental housing portfolio (Public Housing, Multifamily Assisted) and the Department of Agriculture's (USDA) Rural Development Multifamily Programs, as well as rental housing supported through the Low Income Housing Tax Credit (LIHTC). While solar photovoltaic (PV) generation will be the primary renewable energy source utilized under this initiative, solar thermal, wind, geothermal, biomass, combined heat and power, and small-hydro projects, are also included.[213,214,215] Fifty grantees, including 17 Public Housing Authorities (PHAs), had by the summer of 2015 pledged to install renewable energy technologies on-site, totaling 185 MW, enough to power 30,000 homes from solar, geothermal, and combined heat and power systems.[216]

Since the beginning of the Administration, HUD has led the development of many of the Administration's "place-based initiatives," cross-agency efforts to transform the Federal government into a more effective partner for local communities. These collaborative initiatives have led to progress against the challenges facing America's communities partially by taking a more comprehensive approach to community development and focusing on executing locally driven goals. Today over 1,800 communities nation-wide–including cities, towns, counties, and regions–are implementing place-based initiatives. Specifically, HUD is home to the following place-based initiatives:

- The *Promise Zones Initiative* focuses on improving the lives of "middle-class Americans by partnering with local communities and business to create jobs, increase economic security, expand educational opportunities, increase access to quality, affordable housing, and improve public safety."[217,218] Promise Zones continue a line of Federal focus on districts that goes back at least to the Reagan Administration and its interest in Enterprise Zones. HUD has also had a number of programs focused on enabling urban environments, particularly targeted at the most disadvantaged populations. These include a strong traditional focus on public housing programs,[219] including those targeted at improving buildings and housing conditions.
- HUD's Office of Economic Resilience is part of the Partnership for Sustainable Communities shared among HUD, DOT, and EPA. The Office of Economic Resilience helps communities and regions build diverse, prosperous, resilient economies by enhancing quality of place; advancing effective job-creation strategies; reducing housing, transportation, and energy consumption costs; promoting clean-energy solutions; and creating economic opportunities for all. The Office administers three grant programs to help communities achieve these goals: Capacity Building for Sustainable Communities, Sustainable Communities Regional Planning Grants, and Community Challenge Grants.
- The *Strong Cities, Strong Communities Initiative* was launched in July 2011 as an intensive, inter-agency partnership between the Federal Government and local governments in distressed cities. The SC2 concept was developed through engagement with mayors, members of

Congress, foundations, nonprofits and other community partners who are committed to addressing the challenges of local governments. SC2 and its partners are working together to coordinate Federal programs and investments to spark economic growth in distressed areas and create stronger cooperation between community organizations, local leadership, and the federal government. SC2's work has enabled pilot communities to more effectively utilize more than $368 million in existing Federal funds and investments. More significantly, the initiative has succeeded in strengthening local capacity for communities to meet challenges and take advantage of opportunities to grow their economies.

- *The Choice Neighborhoods* program supports locally driven strategies to address struggling neighborhoods with distressed public or HUD-assisted housing through a comprehensive approach to neighborhood transformation. Local leaders, residents, and stakeholders, such as public housing authorities, cities, schools, police, business owners, nonprofits, and private developers, come together to create and implement a plan that transforms distressed HUD housing and addresses the challenges in the surrounding neighborhood. The program is designed to catalyze critical improvements in neighborhood assets, including vacant property, housing, services and schools. Communities must develop a comprehensive neighborhood-revitalization strategy, or Transformation Plan. This Transformation Plan will become the guiding document for the revitalization of the public and/or assisted housing units, while simultaneously directing the transformation of the surrounding neighborhood and positive outcomes for families. Choice administers both Planning and Implementation grants.
- In August 2015, HUD launched the HUD Resource Locator,[220] an innovative mobile app and website to further expand and enhance traditional HUD customer service. The resource locator offers real-time HUD housing information at the fingertips of people looking to quickly connect with building managers, public housing authority representatives, and property management companies to inquire about housing availability and other housing-related questions. The HUD resource locator is one of several services provided by HUD's Enterprise Geographic Information System (eGIS). This tool uses GIS technology to pinpoint where resources are located and allow anyone with a smart-phone or tablet to get relevant contact information. For

example, the new app can be used during a disaster when families need to find housing, or when social service providers are helping persons experiencing homelessness look for available housing assistance. The resource locator uses housing data from HUD and the U.S. Department of Agriculture.

- In December 2015, HUD issued its Assessment Tool to be used by certain HUD program participants to complete their Assessment of Fair Housing (AFH), as part of the guidelines of the recently released Affirmatively Furthering Fair Housing rule. The Assessment Tool equips program participants with the data to identify fair-housing issues and related contributing factors in their jurisdiction and region. The data exposes trends of unequal access to opportunity. It includes datasets such as racially/ethnically concentrated areas of poverty, measures of racial segregation in residential areas, school proficiency index, a low poverty index, a labor-market index, a transit-trips index, a low transportation cost index, and an environmental health index.

Department of Energy Initiatives

The Department of Energy (DOE) has been pursuing research in a number of areas such as green buildings and data centers; building-energy retrofitting; building management; carbon capture, utilization, and storage (CCUS); energy-efficiency technologies; clean air and clean water technologies; waste-treatment technologies; smart grids; and green transportation. In May 2015, DOE unveiled the Better Buildings Solution Center online tool based on 200 solutions that have been implemented and tested over the past four years, when the initiative started.[221]

DOEs *Cities Leading through Energy Analysis and Planning* [222] (Cities-LEAP) project,[223] surveyed 200 U.S. cities and interviewed officials from 20 of these in depth, finding that cities are "challenged to quantify and measure progress towards emissions and energy goals, and would benefit from new tools and methodologies that provide a holistic understanding (across sectors) of energy-related actions or suites or actions in order to prioritize goals." Cities-LEAP also found that cities identified "data and integration of data sets as barriers, [including] data access, transfer of data from utilities, quality of data, using meters and sensors, sub-meters, tools, and models to integrate and combine data."[224]

DOE has plans to go beyond components such as land, buildings, utility networks, or roads to look at city districts as complex systems, such as transportation networks (cars, buses, trains, etc.) that interact in complex feedback loops with other sectors, to look at an integrated understanding of cities and associated metropolitan areas as a whole. This will involve measurements and sensors, computational modeling, and multi-scale analytics, with the particular goal of applying the knowledge gained to specific city decisions.

Environmental Protection Agency

The Environmental Protection Agency (EPA) has programs that can help in funding "green" innovation in districts, with targeted support for the handling of water,[225] storm water, and wastewater as well as air pollution and numerous mechanisms for fostering resilience in cities and other communities. For example, the Water Infrastructure Finance and Innovation Act (WIFIA)[226] Program provides financing for water and wastewater infrastructure. Innovative financing has become available as well through the Water Infrastructure and Resiliency Finance Center[227] established under the Build America Investment Initiative. The Clean Water State Revolving Fund (CWSRF)[228] and the Drinking Water State Revolving Fund (DWSRF)[229] are two Federal-State partnerships that respectively provide communities with financing for a wide range of water quality infrastructure projects and for ensuring safe drinking water.

EPA, along with other Federal agencies, nongovernmental organizations, and private-sector entities, has formed the Green Infrastructure Collaborative to help communities more easily implement green infrastructure.[230] The collaborative members are working to promote green infrastructure with a focus on benefits ranging from improving air quality to reducing energy use to mitigating climate change.

Finally, EPA supports advances in the connected quality of districts and cities through its attention to environmental justice (EJ), defined as "the fair treatment and meaningful involvement of all people regardless of race, color, national origin, or income with respect to the development, implementation, and enforcement of environmental laws, regulations, and policies."[231] The EJ interest can be seen in the Brownfields Program, authorized by the 2002 Small Business Liability Relief and Brownfields Revitalization Act, which targets redevelopment of blighted and other distressed areas through grants and loans that can support clean-up, redevelopment, and job-training.[232]

White House Smart Cities Initiative, NSF, and MetroLab Network

In September 2015, the White House announced a Smart Cities Initiative including new Federal steps and stakeholder collaborations to help communities tackle challenges with technology-driven approaches, in addition to giving greater visibility and coherence to older Federal efforts relevant to innovation in cities. Federal agencies expanded or created technology-based programs, and the launch of the nonprofit MetroLab Network (MLN) was announced. MLN, originating with the City of Pittsburgh and Carnegie Mellon University and now involving at least 20 different city-based collaborations, has attracted private foundation as well as Federal support, fosters collaboration on technical problems among teams of city governments, local universities, and other research institutions and further individual programs are in the planning stage. Its enduring value is in the sharing of successful projects via the coordination of multi-city, multi-university research efforts.[233]

Also as part of the Smart City Initiative, NSF announced a new $35 million in FY 2015 R&D funding (plus another $7.5M in FY 2016) and the Networking and Information Technology Research and Development (NITRD) Program announced a new framework for Smart and Connected Communities[234] to help guide Federal agency investments and foundational research.

APPENDIX D. SELECTED SMART CITIES INTERNATIONAL PROJECTS

Program, City, Country	Organization	Goals
Masdar City Abu Dhabi, United Arab Emirates[235]	Mubadala Development Compay, Government of Abu Dhabi	Masdar is a planned city project in Abu Dhabi, in the United Arab Emirates. Its core is being built by Masdar, a subsidiary of Mubadala Development Company, with the majority of seed capital provided by the Government of Abu Dhabi.

Program, City, Country	Organization	Goals
		Designed by the British architectural firm Foster and Partners, the city relies on solar energy and other renewable energy sources. Masdar City is designed to be a hub for clean tech companies. The first tenant is the Masdar Institute of Science and Technology, a university partnership with MIT's Technology and Development Program.
Amsterdam Smart City Project, Amsterdam, Netherlands[236]	City of Amsterdam with 100+ partners	Amsterdam Smart City (ASC) is a unique partnership between companies, governments, knowledge institutions and the people of Amsterdam. It is a frontrunner in the development of Amsterdam as a smart city. Where social and technological infrastructures and solutions facilitate and accelerate sustainable economic growth, improving the quality of life in the city for everyone. ASC believes in a habitable city where it is pleasant to both live and work. In six years ASC has grown into a platform with over 100 partners, which are involved in more than 90 innovative projects.
Andorra Living Lab, Andorra[237]	Actua Tech Foundation, MIT Media Lab	Collaboration between the Andorran government and the MIT Media Lab to developing a living lab to test the use of data for addressing urban design, tourism, and innovation for the country of Andorra. Actua Tech is a partnership between Andorra Telecom and FEDA (National Utility Company).
Smart City Barcelona, Spain[238]	City of Barcelona	Smart-city areas include public and social services, environment, mobility, companies and business, research and innovation, communications, infrastructure, tourism, citizen cooperation, and international projects.
Smart Cities, China[239]	Ministry of Housing and Urban-Rural Development (MoHURD)	103 cities, districts, and towns in China have been earmarked by the Ministry of Housing and Urban-Rural Development to be developed into smart cities this year.

Appendix D. (Continued)

Program, City, Country	Organization	Goals
		In an effort to promote urbanization and boost the national economy at a time when China's GDP growth has experienced a recent slide, the ministry is looking to transform cities combining government investments, modern infrastructure, and information technology to make them more competitive. The ministry is calling for the listed cities to issue detailed proposals about how they will begin reconstruction within an overall design plan.
HafenCity Project, Hamburg, Germany[240]	Port of Hamburg, HafenCity Corporation, HafenCity University, MIT Media Lab	Cooperation agreement between the HafenCity University and the MIT Media Lab to develop smart cities planning in the HafenCity District (Port of Hamburg) and neighboring districts. Projects include use of urban data analytics to create interactive city planning tools.
Smart Cities, India[241]	Office of the Prime Minister of India	The Indian government plans to identify 20 smart cities in 2015, 40 in 2016 and another 40 in 2017. The 100 potential smart cities nominated by all the states and union territories based on stage 1 criteria will prepare smart city plans which will be evaluated in stage 2 of the competition for prioritizing cities for financing. In the first round of this stage, 20 top scorers will be chosen for financing during the initial financial year. The remaining will be asked to make up the deficiencies identified by the Apex Committee in the Ministry of Urban Development for participation in the next two rounds of competition. 40 cities each will be selected for financing during the next rounds of competition.
Rise Prize, India[242]	Mahindra	Mahindra to fund two Challenges: (1) Solar, (2) Driverless Car, one Million Dollars

Program, City, Country	Organization	Goals
Songdo, Korea[243]	Government of Korea, Gale International, Posco, Morgan Stanley	Songdo International Business District (Songdo IBD) is a new smart city or "ubiquitous city" built from scratch on 600 hectares (1,500 acres) of reclaimed land along Incheon's waterfront, 65 kilometres (40 mi) southwest of Seoul, South Korea and connected to Incheon International Airport by a 12.3-kilometre (7.6 mi) reinforced concrete highway bridge, called Incheon Bridge. Along with Yeongjong and Cheongna, it is part of the Incheon Free Economic Zone.
MK: Smart Initiative, Milton Keynes, UK[244]	City of Milton Keynes	MK: Smart is a large collaborative initiative, partly funded by HEFCE (the Higher Education Funding Council for England) and led by The Open University, which will develop innovative solutions to support economic growth in Milton Keynes. Central to the project is the creation of a state-of-the-art 'MK Data Hub' which will support the acquisition and management of vast amounts of data relevant to city systems from a variety of data sources. These will include data about energy and water consumption, transport data, data acquired through satellite technology, social and economic datasets, and crowdsourced data from social media or specialized apps.
Catapult Driverless Vehicle Project, UK[245]	Innovate UK	Intelligent Mobility project using self-driving technologies for people and goods movement.
Smart Nation, Singapore[246]	Programme Office in the Prime Minister's Office	The Smart Nation initiative adopts a people-centric approach by rallying citizens, industries, research institutions, and the government to co-create innovative solutions. Major applications of the Smart Nation include Smart Mobility and Smart Living.

Appendix D. (Continued)

Program, City, Country	Organization	Goals
Lee Kuan Yew Centre for Livable Cities, Singapore[247]	Singapore University of Technology and Design	The Lee Kuan Yew Centre for Innovative Cities (LKY CIC) at the Singapore University of Technology and Design (SUTD) focuses on the integrated use of technology, design and policy to study solutions for cities. The LKY CIC works with architects, designers, engineers, social scientists, and urban planners to understand the complex and critical issues of urbanisation, and to explore sustainable and innovative urban solutions.
Singapore-MIT Alliance for Research and Technology (SMART), Singapore[248]	MIT, Government of Singapore	The Singapore-MIT Alliance for Research and Technology (SMART) is a major research enterprise established by the Massachusetts Institute of Technology (MIT) in partnership with the National Research Foundation of Singapore (NRF) in 2007. Research areas include: BioSystems and Micromechanics, Environmental Sensing and Modeling,Infectious Diseases, Future Urban Mobility, and Low Energy Electronic Systems.
Kista Science City, Stockholm, Sweden[249]	Krista Science City AB	Kista Science City is a creative melting pot in Stockholm where companies, researchers and students collaborate in order to develop and grow. The foremost sector in Kista is ICT (Information and Communication Technology). Kista Science City AB is a wholly-owned subsidiary of the Electrum Foundation and an operative, non-profit organisation. The goal is to make Kista Science City a place where people and business can continue to develop. Strong cooperation between business, academia and the public sector is encouraged in order to ensure continued growth in Kista Science City.

Program, City, Country	Organization	Goals
Smart City at TAF (Taiwan Air Force), Taipei, Taiwan[250]	Office of the Premier of Taiwan, MIT Media Lab	Collaboration between the Office of the Premier of Taiwan and the MIT Media Lab to develop Living Lab experiments at the former Taiwan Air Force (TAF) base in central Taipei. Experiments include low-speed, self-driving vehicles as well as urban innovation incubators.

APPENDIX E. TOOLS FOR URBAN DEVELOPMENT DISTRICTS

City dashboards that utilize data feeds from open and closed sources have become increasingly common within city governments. Mayors use them as a barometer of urban performance across many dimensions including levels of congestion, pollution, crime, noise, waste, and even pothole repairs. Although some are open source and accessible to anyone with an Internet connection, these tools are typically designed for experts, are often one off solutions, utilize only low-resolution data, and do not fully utilize standards to enable scaling. Cities attempting to regenerate neighborhoods have begun to invest in Innovation Districts, in some cases empowered with special economic zone status. This presents a new opportunity for cities to leverage urban data (e.g., through the City Web) to create a new set of tools that can be applied to Urban Development Districts (UDDs) to maximize their benefit. The CityScope project developed by the City Science Initiative at MIT Media Lab is a data-driven, interactive, tangible, 3D urban observatory and urban decision support system (DSS) designed to engage non-expert stakeholders for city development.

As a three-dimensional urban observatory the CityScope combines physical scale models (made of LEGO bricks) and 3D projections of urban digital data to form a hybrid physical-virtual reality platform that enables multiple stakeholders to engage in urban decision-making. The CityScope has two modes of interaction. The first is passive observation and the second is active, participatory planning. In observation mode, the CityScope visualizes urban data sets, real-time traffic flows, and social media as well as simulated data such as energy consumption or solar access, so that the users can toggle between information layers (see Figure 1). This allows users of the CityScope to identify potential challenges and opportunities when optimizing existing urban systems.

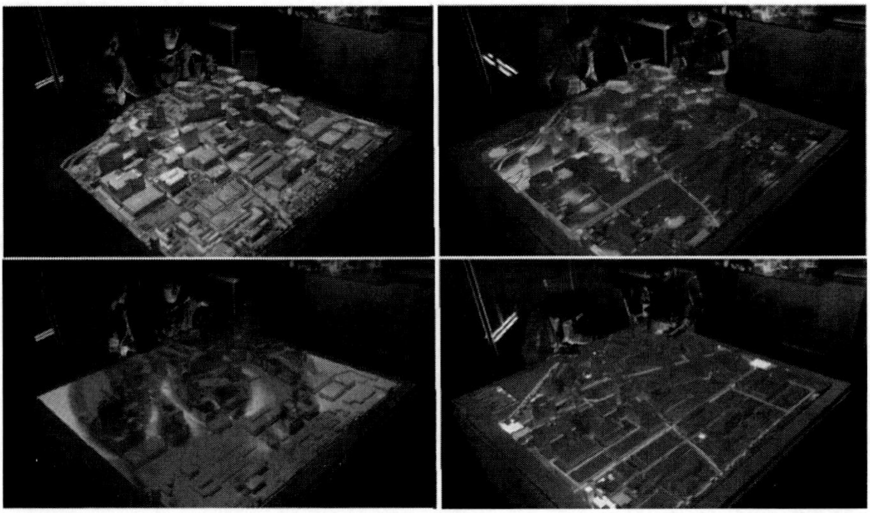

Figure 1. CityScope with satellite data, Twitter user activity, wind flow simulation, and mobility networks (clockwise starting from upper left).

In active mode, the CityScope allows users to physically move elements of the platform (such as buildings or roads) to simulate alternative urban outcomes. For example, if a user moves buildings onto an empty site, then the CityScope will visualize the corresponding increase in the population density and the effects on traffic, energy use, and the demand on city services (see Figure 2).

Figure 2. CityScope Interactive platform.

Working with the City of Boston and the Barr Foundation, the Media Lab customized the CityScope to address the problems of transportation access in the historically disadvantaged neighborhood of Dudley Square in Roxbury, Massachusetts. The project was built upon a previous study conducted by Barr on the deployment of new Bus Rapid Transit (BRT) lines for the City of Boston, including a new line that would intersect through Dudley Square. BRT systems typically cost a fraction (approximately one-tenth) of subway lines and comparable throughput efficiencies of 50-60%. The introduction of BRT would vastly improve commute times, job access, and the overall quality of life for Roxbury residents, although a dedicated lane would need to be created in order to maximize these benefits. A tool was needed to engage transportation planners, city officials, transit agencies, and most importantly the citizens themselves that would allow the community to co-create a new transportation system while understanding all of the trade-offs.

BRT systems operate efficiently because dedicated lanes provide congestion-free access and travel priority to the riders of mass transit; they displace regular travel lanes (for private cars and trucks) thus increasing travel times for automobiles. BRT systems also utilize enclosed pre-pay stations, which allow for improved boarding and disembarking times. These stations are also elevated, to allow for fast handicap access. These components help to reduce the bus-stacking problem (built up delays that bunch up buses). The CityScope developed for Dudley Square was divided into three components to address these trade-offs at the regional, neighborhood, and street scale.

The CityScope, at the regional scale, allows users to enter points of interest (home, work, shopping, etc.) and to compare their commute under today's transit system and what it would be with the new BRT line (see Figure 3). It also allows participants to visualize increased job and housing access. At the neighborhood scale, users were able to visualize the impact of new stations (location, walking distance), dedicate lane routing, and capital and operational costs (Figure 4). Finally, the street scale CityScope allowed users to visualize the trade-offs between standard bus systems, improved bus systems, and gold-standard BRT systems including boarding times, total commute times, parking spaces eliminated, travel time for automobiles, etc. (also Figure 4). This set of new tools was designed to work in concert with key stakeholders from the community, non-governmental organizations, government, and planners to engage in constructive discussion, and to encourage participation through new technology. By developing an understanding of BRT concepts, trade-offs, and impacts, users can use these tools to design their own proposals and thus contribute their own ideas for future scenario planning.

Figure 3. CityScope at the regional scale (left) and neighborhood (right).

Figure 4. CityScope at the neighborhood scale interaction (left) and street scale (right).

APPENDIX F. A VISION FOR OLDER ADULTS IN CITIES

Most developed nations have an aging population, a combination of greater life expectancy and lower fertility rates. Globally, the number of individuals over 60 is expected to more than double as soon as 2050, to more than two billion. The majority of those will live in cities.

Many people see this as a gloomy policy challenge, leading inevitably to "debt, disease and despair" in the words of Paul Irving, of the Milken Institute. But in the same article, focused on the "Action Plan for Successful Aging" in Singapore, he proposes an alternative viewpoint, paraphrased as follows: Increasing life span can be a positive force for economic and social opportunity, enhanced cohesion and intergenerational harmony. Older adults represent a massive human capital asset waiting for a call to action, and a growing consumer market. We need to maximize the promise of disease prevention and wellness to extend health span and lessen the impact of disability on productivity and quality of life. Technology can help us do this, and if we do the longevity dividend confers abundant possibilities.

Cities can provide the ideal environment to make good on this more optimistic promise of successful aging, for individuals and for society, as well as providing the supports and comforts people need at the end the life. The same factors that can make the city of the future more green, mobile, and connected or inclusive can combine to make the city a good place for older people.

Cities can be very attractive places to live one's older years. Cities in their current form ideally can offer rich cultural environments, easier transportation, availability of delivery services, and opportunities to develop new as well as ongoing and enriching social networks, such as through senior centers, cultural organizations and religious communities. Social interaction has been shown to be a key determinant of maintaining cognitive and functional heath.

As a result of these factors, many cities are experiencing an influx of empty nesters, who are downsizing and choosing the convenience of urban living. Other cities already have large numbers of older people who are aging in place, which can create "naturally occurring retirement communities." Cities offer the population density and efficiencies of scale that support successful aging.

But it could be so much better, enhanced by the policies driving greener, mobile, and connected cities.

Green

Older people are vulnerable to environmental pollutants, especially airborne particulates. Respiratory conditions, such as chronic obstructive lung disease, are common for this population, and exacerbations can lead to disability, limited ability to be outside and to exercise, and avoidable hospitalizations. All of those lead to accelerated frailty and isolation. The environmental conditions for cities can be improved by redesigning the built environment. Ideal built environments can encourage physical activity for everyone, which also will benefit elders as walking is an excellent form of exercise, with demonstrated impact on vitality, mood, sleep, strength, as well as cognitive function. Furthermore, the built environment can encourage intergenerational interactions, more vibrant communities, and more active engagement for older people, even those with some degree of disability.

Mobile

Many older adults have diminishing abilities to drive, and having affordable alternatives allows them to maintain their independence. For many older people, mobility is further limited by physical or medical conditions. In cities today, buses, light rail, subways, and—for those who can afford it—taxis are options when driving is no longer an option. Older people in urban areas generally have many more options than for people living in suburbia. Walkable neighborhoods also can allow people to get around without driving, especially if those neighborhoods are intergenerational, inclusive of opportunities for intellectual and social engagement, free of crime and have option for people to easily access transportation.

An age-friendly city of the future would have additional transportation options. Autonomous vehicles could be summoned through mobile devices and tablets, thereby safely and inexpensively transporting people. Shared rides could be exchanged through online platforms that would also provide social connectedness. And more mass-transit options could be available with real-time arrival technology (so that people do not have to wait in the cold or heat).

As people live longer, some will want—and others will need—to continue gainful employment. Mobility gives an older person more options for flexible work, inside or outside the home, contributing to one's sense of self and to the economy at the same time. It also gives employers more ability to hire older workers on flexible time schedules with workable transportation arrangements.

Connected

Older adults benefit from social engagement as they age, which can help them maintain cognitive capacities and prevent depression, a significant (30% prevalence in older adults) and debilitating disorder that is both preventable and treatable. The American Association of Retired Persons (AARP) studies demonstrate that self-reported loneliness is extremely common and predictive of higher rates of illness and hospital use. Isolation is a problem as most older people in the United States do not live in close proximity to family members. Internet-mediated communications, health monitoring, and easy sharing of experiences strengthen families, create opportunities for interaction with others, and allow the older persons to continue to live independently while being in close touch with children and grandchildren.

In the city of the future, access to broadband and Internet-mediated activity would be widely available. Cities would leverage this by offering easy access to training and technology trouble shooting. This could be done with volunteers from high schools, who would also strengthen the intergenerational connections. But some innovative cities have engaged tech-savvy elders who volunteer their time or are paid for providing a public service. Connectedness can be expanded by virtual senior centers such as New York City's Older Adults Technology Services (OATS) that can connect adults to cultural attractions and other nearby adults, training for older adults in computer skills so they can take greater advantage of online services, and internet-mediated services that allow them to identify volunteer opportunities.[251]

Health care services can be offered through telehealth and telemedicine. This means health care will be seamlessly available through Skype-like services, which will minimize unnecessary transportation and allow more time for social or employment related activities. Easy access to an answer to questions or concerns can also help identify a medical problem that needs attention, such as reassuring someone that he or she does not need immediate medical attention. Remote monitoring technologies can watch for falls (and assess fall risk), eating and sleeping habits, and other health related factors. These can can be unobtrusive, respect privacy and permission requirements, and provide important predictive information to enhance safety.

Summary

Many U.S. cities are seeking to become age-friendly, with a global movement organized by the World Health Organization (WHO). The New York Academy of Medicine and AARP are organizing communities across the United States. These cities range from New York City to Macon, Georgia to Des Moines, Iowa to Portland, Oregon. Most of the innovations of age-friendly cities have not focused on technology, but have focused on community resources, built environments, and public programs. The lessons learned by these cities can be spread more broadly with technology innovations that support green, fluid, and connected cities.

As one noted gerontologist said, a society that is good for elders is a society that is good for everyone.

Accordingly, improving cities for older adults will benefit not just older adults but all people that live and work there.

Appendix G. Additional Experts Providing Input

Andrew Abrams
Chief
Transportation Branch
Office of Management and Budget

Rohit Aggarwala
Professor
School of International and Public Affairs
Columbia University
Principal at Bloomberg Associates

Jose M. Baptista
Vice President, Platform Services Operations
100 Resilient Cities
Rockefeller Foundation

Eran Ben-Joseph
Professor and Department Head
Department of Urban Studies and Planning MIT

Austin Brown
Senior Policy Analyst for Energy R&D
Office of Science and Technology Policy

Kevin Bush
Senior Analyst
Office of Public and Indian Housing
Department of Housing and Urban Development

Nicholas Chim
Co-Founder
Flux

Peter Chipman
Senior Sustainability Officer
Office of Federal Sustainability
Council of Environmental Quality

Elizabeth Cocke
Director
Affordable Housing
Research and Technology Division
Department of Housing and Urban Development

Daniel Correa
Senior Advisor for Innovation Policy
Office of Science and Technology Policy

Joseph Coughlin
Director
MIT AgeLab

Matthew Dalbey
Office Director
Office of Sustainable Communities
Environmental Protection Agency

Ankur Datta
Senior Policy Advisory
Department of Treasury

Linda Dodge
Chief of Staff
Intelligent Transportation Systems Joint
Program Office
Department of Transportation

Kevin Dopart
Program Manager
Connected Vehicle Safety and Automation
Department of Transportation

Mark Dowd
Deputy Assistant Secretary for Research and Technology
Senior Advisor to the Secretary Department of Transportation

Kerry Duggan
Assistant Director for Policy
Office of the Vice President

Michelle Enger
Chief
Housing Branch
Office of Management and Budget

Michael Flowers
Urban Science Fellow
Center for Urban Science and Progress
New York University

Andrey Fradkin
Postdoctoral Fellow
National Bureau of Economic Research

Salin Geevarghese
Deputy Assistant Secretary for International and Philanthropic Innovation
Department of Housing and Urban Development

Erwin Gianchandani
Acting Deputy Assistant Director
Computer and Information Science and Engineering Directorate
National Science Foundation

Stacey Gillett
Government Innovation
What Works Cities Initiative
Bloomberg Philanthropies

Edward Glaeser
Fred Eleanor Glimp Professor of Economics
Department of Economics
Harvard University

Maggie Goodrich
Chief Information Officer
Public Safety
Los Angeles Police Department and Los
Angeles Fire Department

Christopher Greer
Director
Smart Grid and Cyber-Physical Systems
Program Office
National Coordinator for Smart Grid
Interoperability
National Institute of Standards and Technology

Richard Gunn
Chief Executive Officer
Project Frog

Jonathan Hall
Head of Policy Research
Uber Technologies

Jed Hermann
Senior Advisor to the CEO
Corporation for National and Community Services

Peter Hirshberg
Chairman
City Innovate Foundation

Kent Hiteshew
Director
Office of State and Local Finance
Department of Treasury

Michael Holland
Chief of Staff
Center for Urban Science and Progress
New York University

Scot Horst
Chief Product Officer
U.S. Green Building council

Maggie Hsu Advisor
Downtown Project

Calvin Johnson
Deputy Assistant Secretary
Office of Research, Evaluation, and Monitoring
Department of Housing and Urban Development

Mark Johnson
Director
Advanced Manufacturing Office
Department of Energy

Courtney Jones
Special Assistant
Office of Policy Development and Research
Department of Housing and Urban Development

Lucy Jones
Science Advisor for Risk Reduction
U.S. Geological Survey
Special Advisor to the Mayor of Los Angeles on Resilience

Marcia Kadanoff
Chief Strategy Officer
City innovate Foundation

Ian Kalin
Chief Data Officer
Department of Commerce

Richard Kauffman
Senior Advisor to the Secretary of Energy
Department of Energy

Clifton Kellogg
Executive Director
Detroit Working Group
Office of Management and Budget

Vinod Khosla
Founder
Khosla Ventures

Constantine Kontokosta
Deputy Director, Academics
Assistant Professor of Urban Informatics
Center for Urban Science and Progress
New York University

Khee Poh Lam
Project Director
Carnegie Mellon University
Consortium for Building Energy Innovation

Hans Larsen
Former Director
Department of Transportation
City of San Jose

Kent Larson
Principal Research Scientist
MIT Media Lab

Jonathan Levin
Holbrook Working Professor of Price Theory
Department of Economics
Stanford University

Benjamin Levine
Interim Director
MetroLab Network

Jonathan Levy
Deputy Chief of Staff
Department of Energy

Nathaniel Loewentheil
Senior Policy Advisor
National Economic Council

John MacWilliams
Associate Deputy Secretary
Department of Energy

Celinda Marsh
Program Examiner
Science and Space Branch
Office of Management and Budget

Tara McGuinness
Senior Advisor
Directors Office
Office of Management and Budget

Matthew McKenna
Advisor
United States Department of Agriculture

Carlos Monje
Acting Under Secretary of Transportation for Policy
Assistant Secretary for Transportation Policy
Department of Transportation

Daniel Morgan
Chief Data Officer
Department of Transportation

Jayne Morrow
Former Executive Director
National Science and Technology Council
Office of Science and Technology Policy

Katherine O'Regan
Assistant Secretary for Policy Development and Research
Department of Housing and Urban Development

Franklin Orr
Under Secretary for Science and Energy
Department of Energy

Timothy Papandreou
Director
Office of Innovation
San Francisco Municipal Transportation Agency

DJ Patil
Chief Data Scientist
Office of Science and Technology Policy

Aristides Patrinos
Deputy Director for Research
Center for Urban Science and Progress
New York University

Robert Pepper
Vice President
Global Technology Policy
Cisco Systems, Inc.

Marcia Pincus
Program Manager
Environment (AERIS) and ITS evaluation
Department of Transportation

Balaji Prabhakar
Chief Scientist and Co-Founder
Urban Engines
Professor of Computer Science and Electrical Engineering
Stanford University

Seleta Reynolds
General Manager
Los Angeles Department of Transportation

Sokwoo Rhee
Associate Director
Cyber-Physical Systems Program
National Institute of Standards and Technology

Andrew Right
Executive Director
Build America Transportation Investment Center
Department of Transportation

Caroline Rodier
Associate Director
Urban Land Use and Transportation Center
University of California, Davis

Paul Romer
Professor of Economics
Director
The Urbanization Project New York University

Amir Roth
Technology Manager
Building Technologies Office
Office of Energy Efficiency & Renewable Energy
Department of Energy

Brent Ryan
Associate Professor
Urban Planning Program MIT

Kamran Saddique
Chief Executive Officer
City Innovate Foundation

Janette Sadik-Khan
Principal
Transportation
Bloomberg Associates

Robert Sampson
Henry Ford II Professor of the Social Sciences
Director
Boston Area Research Initiative
Harvard University

Katy Sartorius
Special Advisor
Department of Energy

Joel Scheraga
Senior Advisor for Climate Adaptation
Office of Policy
Environmental Protection Agency

Tarak Shah
Senior Advisor to the Under Secretary for Science and Energy
Department of Energy

Egan Smith
Managing Director
Intelligent Transportation System
Joint Program Office
Department of Transportation

Jeffrey Brian Straubel
Co-Founder and Chief Technology Officer
Tesla Motors

Arun Sundararajan
Professor of Information, Operations and
Management Sciences
Leonard N. Stern School of Business
New York University

Luke Tate
Special Assistant to the President for Economic Mobility
White House Domestic Policy Council

Sebastian Thrun
Research Professor
Stanford University

Harriet Tregoning
Principal Deputy Assistant Security
Office of Community Planning and
Development Resilience
Department of Housing of Urban Development

Christopher Urmson
Director
Self-Driving Cars
X

Aden Van Noppen
Advisor to the Chief Technology Officer
Office of Science and Technology Policy

Sarah Wartell
President
Urban Institute

Geoffrey West
Distinguished Professor and Past President
Santa Fe Institute

John Williams
Director of Innovation and Technology
Office of Innovation and Technology
Small Business Administration

Sir Alan Wilson
Professor of Urban and Regional Systems

Centre for Advanced Spatial Analysis
University College London

Brian Worth
Federal Public Policy Manager
Uber

Elizabeth Yee
Vice President, Strategic Partnerships and Solutions
100 Resilient Cities
Rockefeller Foundation

David Yeh
Consultant
Performance and Personnel Management
Division
Office of Management and Budget

Corinna Zarek
Senior Advisor to the Chief Technology Officer
for Open government
Office of Science and Technology Policy

Daniel Zarrilli
Director
Mayor's office of Recovery and Resiliency
Mayor's office of Sustainability
New York City

Additional Acknowledgments

Viktoria Gisladottir
PCAST Spring 2015 Intern

Zeyi Lin
PCAST Fall 2015 Intern

Jonathan Gheur
Principal
Signature Creative

Lindsay Gorman
PCAST Fall 2014 Intern

Carlton Reeves
PCAST Summer 2015 Intern

About the President's Council of Advisors on Science and Technology

The President's Council of Advisors on Science and Technology (PCAST) is an advisory group of the Nation's leading scientists and engineers, appointed by the President to augment the science and technology advice available to him from inside the White House and from cabinet departments and other Federal agencies. PCAST is consulted about, and often makes policy recommendations concerning, the full range of issues where understandings from the domains of science, technology, and innovation bear potentially on the policy choices before the President.

The President's Council of Advisors on Science and Technology

Co-Chairs

John P. Holdren
Assistant to the President for Science and Technology
Director, Office of Science and Technology Policy

Eric S. Lander
President
Broad Institute of Harvard and MIT

Vice Chairs

William Press
Raymer Professor in Computer Science and Integrative Biology
University of Texas at Austin

Maxine Savitz
General Manager (retired)
Honeywell

Members

Wanda M. Austin
President and CEO
The Aerospace Corporation

Rosina Bierbaum
Professor, School of Natural Resources and Environment
University of Michigan

Christine Cassel
President and CEO
National Quality Forum

Christopher Chyba
Professor, Astrophysical Sciences and
International Affairs
Director, Program on Science
and Global Security
Princeton University

S. James Gates, Jr.
John S. Toll Professor of Physics
Director, Center for String
and Particle Theory
University of Maryland, College Park

Mark Gorenberg
Managing Member
Zetta Venture Partners

Susan L. Graham
Pehong Chen Distinguished Professor
Emerita in Electrical Engineering and Computer Science
University of California, Berkeley

Michael McQuade
Senior Vice President for Science and Technology
United Technologies Corporation

Chad Mirkin
George B. Rathmann Professor of Chemistry
Director, International Institute for Nanotechnology
Northwestern University

Mario Molina
Distinguished Professor, Chemistry and Biochemistry
University of California, San Diego
Professor, Center for Atmospheric Sciences
Scripps Institution of Oceanography

Craig Mundie
President
Mundie & Associates

Ed Penhoet
Director
Alta Partners
Professor Emeritus, Biochemistry and Public Health
University of California, Berkeley

Barbara Schaal
Dean of the Faculty of Arts and Sciences
Mary-Dell Chilton Distinguished Professor of Biology
Washington University of St. Louis

Eric Schmidt
Executive Chairman
Alphabet

Daniel Schrag
Sturgis Hooper Professor of Geology
Professor, Environmental Science and Engineering
Director, Harvard University Center for Environment
Harvard University

Staff

Marjory S. Blumenthal
Executive Director

Jennifer L. Michael
Program Support Specialist

Diana E. Pankevich
AAAS Science & Technology Policy Fellow

Ashley Predith
Assistant Executive Director

PCAST Cities Working Group

Working Group members participated in the preparation of an initial draft of this report. Those working group members who are not PCAST members are not responsible for, nor necessarily endorse, the final version of this report as modified and approved by PCAST.

Co-Chairs

Mark Gorenberg*
Managing Member
Zetta Venture Partners

Craig Mundie*
President
Mundie Associates

Eric Schmidt*
Executive Chairman
Alphabet

Working Group Members

Adrian Aoun
Director
Special Projects Google,
Alphabet

Luis Bettencourt
Professor of Complex Systems
Santa Fe Institute

Rosina Bierbaum*
Professor, School of Natural Resources
and Environment
University of Michigan

Christine Cassel*
President and CEO
National Quality Forum

Ryan C.C. Chin,
Managing Director and Research Scientist
City Science Initiative
MIT Media Lab

Charles Catlett
Senior Computer Scientist
Argonne National Laboratory and
University of Chicago
Director, Urban Center for Computation and Data

Daniel Doctoroff
Chairman and CEO
Sidewalk Labs

S. James Gates, Jr.*
John S. Toll Professor of Physics
Director, Center for String and
Particle Theory
University of Maryland, College Park

Susan L. Graham*
Pehong Chen Distinguished Professor
Emerita in Electrical Engineering and Computer Science
University of California, Berkeley

Steven Koonin
Director
Center for Urban Science and Progress
New York University

Richard G. Luthy
Silas H. Palmer Professor
Civil and Environmental Engineering
Stanford University

Peter Marx
Chief Technology Officer
City of Los Angeles
Adjunct Professor
University of Southern California,
Los Angeles

William Press*
Raymer Professor in Computer Science and
Integrative Biology
University of Texas at Austin

Maxine Savitz*
General Manager (retired) Honeywell

Daniel Schrag*
Sturgis Hooper Professor of Geology
Professor, Environmental Science and Engineering
Director, Harvard University Center for Environment
Harvard University

Joseph Stagner
Executive Director
Sustainability and Energy management
Stanford University

Nancy Sutley
Chief Sustainability and Economic Development Officer
Los Angeles Department of Water and Power

Staff

Marjory S. Blumenthal
Executive Director

Jennifer L. Michael
Program Support Specialist

Diana E. Pankevich
AAAS Science & Technology Policy Fellow

Ashley Predith
Assistant Executive Director

*denotes PCAST member

End Notes

[1] The first urban planning courses appeared in the United States and UK in 1909. www-personal.umich.edu/~sdcamp/up540/timeline12.html.

[2] Lucy Westcott. "More Americans moving to cities, reversing the suburban exodus," *The Wire*, 2014. www.thewire.com/national/2014/03/more-americans-moving-to-cities-reversing-the-suburban-exodus/359714.

[3] "Urban renewal? Census figures show cities surging," *U.S. News, 2013.* usnews.nbcnews.com/news/2013/05/23/18441345-urban-renewal-census-figures-show-cities-surging.

[4] Detroit Future City. detroitfuturecity.com/wp-content/uploads/2015/01/Eco-D-4.pdf.

[5] "AAA study finds costs associated with traffic crashes are more than three times greater than congestion costs," 2011. newsroom.aaa.com/2011/11/aaa-study-finds-costs-associated-with-traffic-crashes-are-more-than-three-times-greaterthan-congestion-costs.

[6] "Economic and environmental impact of traffic congestion in Europe and the US," *INRIX*, 2014. Inrix.com/wpcontent/uploads/2015/08/Whitepaper Cebr-Cost-of-Congestion.pdf.

[7] "The hidden health costs of transportation," *American Public Health Association*, 2010. www.apha.org/~/media/files/pdf/factsheets/hidden health costs transportation.ashx.

[8] From a 2005 analysis: For example, in incorporated Los Angeles County, there are 18.6 million parking spaces accounting for 14% of all land, but the amount of space dedicated to parking in the central business district in Los Angeles is a staggering 81% (including multi-level parking structures); the numbers are also high in other cities—25% and 31% in Phoenix's and San Francisco's respective central business districts. 30% of LA traffic in the central business district is just due to people looking for parking spaces. Manville, M. and D. Shoup. "Parking, People, and Cities." *J. Urban PLann.Dev. 2005. shoup.bol.ucla.edu/People,Parking,CitiesJUPD.pdf.*

[9] Spieser, et al. "Toward a systematic approach to the design and evaluation of automated mobility on demand systems a case study in Singapore," *Massachusetts Institute of Technology,* 2014. Dspace.mit.edu/handle/1721.1/82904.

[10] For example see: www.nature.com/nclimate/journal/v5/n9/full/nclimate2685.html; link.springer.com/chapter/10.1007/978-3-319-05990-713; and www.nrel.gov/docs/fy15 osti/63739.pdf.

[11] See: onlinepubs.trb.org/Onlinepubs/tcrp/tcrp syn 115.pdf.

[12] U.S. Department of Transportation Intelligent Transportation Systems, Joint Program Office. www.its.dot.gov.

[13] See: www.thelocal.dk/20150202/copenhagen-to-roll-out-new-smart-traffic-systems; www.fiercewireless.com/europe/story/here-moves-pilot-lte-based-intelligent-transport-system/2015-10-07; www.seeits.eu/docs/Related/national action plans/ITS report UK annexes%20(en).pdf.

[14] Jason Margolis. "In Michigan, a testing ground for a future of driverless cars," *NPR*, 2015. www.npr.org/sections/alltechconsidered/2015/07/31/427733153/in-michigan-a-testing-ground-for-a-future-of-driverlesscars.

[15] "Energy-efficient buildings: heating and cooling equipment roadmaps," *International Energy Agency*, 2011. www.iea.org/publications/freepublications/publication/buildings roadmap.pdf; "District energy in cities," *United Nations Environment Programme*, 2015. www.unep.org/energy/districtenergyincities.

[16] Stanford Energy System Innovations. sustainable.stanford.edu/campus-action/stanford-energy-system-innovations-sesi.

[17] Cole Mellino. "4 U.S. cities that have gone 100% renewable," *EcoWatch*, 2015. ecowatch.com/2015/11/19/cities-100- renewable-energy.

[18] Cassandra Profita. "Portland now generating hydropower in its water pipes," *Oregon Public Broadcasting*, 2015. www.opb.org/news/article/portland-now-generating-hydropower-in-its-water-pipes.

[19] Department of Energy Global Energy Storage Database. www.energystorageexchange.org/projects.

[20] LEED is a green-building certification program that recognizes best-in-class building strategies and practices. To receive LEED certification, building projects satisfy prerequisites and earn points to achieve different levels of certification. Prerequisites and credits differ for each rating system. www.usgbc.org/leed.

[21] It includes efficient mechanical, lighting, and envelope systems, a district combined heat and power plant, municipally supplied reclaimed water for irrigation, and water-efficient fixtures, as well as building materials, furniture, and cleaning products, and pest management procedures based on rigorous health and sustainability standards. "Green building city market briefs," *U.S. Green Building Council*, 2015. www.usgbc.org/resources/green-building-city-market-briefs.

[22] Ibid., 12.

[23] "Buried no longer: confronting America's water infrastructure challenge," *American Water Works Association*, 2011. www.awwa.org/Portals/0/files/legreg/documents/Buried No Longer.pdf; "2013 Report card for America's infrastructure," *American Society of Civil Engineers*, 2013. www.infrastructurereportcard.org/ a/#p/drinking-water/overview.

[24] "Using graywater and stormwater to enhance local water supplies: as assessment of risks, costs, and benefits," *National Academies Press,* 2016, p19-20. www.nap.edu/catalog/21866/using-graywater-and-stormwater-to-enhance-local-watersupplies-an.

[25] Ibid., 50-51.

[26] Detroit Future City. detroitfuturecity.com/wp-content/uploads/2015/01/Eco-D-4.pdf.

[27] "Using graywater and stormwater to enhance local water supplies: as assessment of risks, costs, and benefits," *National Academies Press,* 2016, p21-22.

[28] "Experiments Advance Gardening at Home and in Space," *Spinoff,* NASA. spinoff.nasa.gov/Spinoff2008/ch 3.html.

[29] Aerofarms. aerofarms.com.

[30] C.J. Hughes, "In Newark, a vertical indoor farm helps anchor an area's revival," *The New York Times,* 2015. www.nytimes.com/2015/04/08/realestate/commercial/in-newark-a-vertical-indoor-farm-helps-anchor-an-areasrevival.html? r=2.

[31] Gotham Greens. gothamgreens.com/our-farms.

[32] "Making room for housing and jobs," *Pratt Center for Community Development*, 2015. prattcenter.net/research/makingroom-housing-and-jobs.

[33] Nathan Donato-Weinstein. "Lennar buying 100 acres as developers encircle Fremont's new BART station, "Silicon Valley Business Journal, 2014. www.bizjournals.com/sanjose/news/2014/06/02/lennar-buying-100-acres-from-union-pacificas.html.

[34] Pratt Center for Community Development prattcenter.net/equitable-innovation-economies.

[35] Bruce Katz and Julie Wagner. "The Rise of Innovation Districts," *The Brookings Institute,* 2014. www.brookings.edu/about/programs/metro/innovation-districts.

[36] See: www.usgbc.org/articles/getting-know-leed-neighborhood-development.

[37] See: ecodistricts.org/target-cities.

[38] See: www.mckinsey.com/insights/sustainability/building the cities of the future with green districts.

[39] See: www.sfclimateaction.org.

[40] See: largelots.org.

[41] See: makeloveland.com.

[42] According to the American Community Survey indicate that 86% of Americans commuted to work using a car or truck and that 76% drove alone. www.census.gov/prod/2011pubs/acs-15.pdf.

[43] There are other kinds of technology use, such as the combination of open data and smartphones to help people optimize their use of public transit—technology that can also contribute to transportation-related planning.

[44] McKinsey estimated as much as 50 to 80 percent less private vehicle kilometers traveled may be possible. www.mckinsey.com/insights/sustainability/building the cities of the future with green districts.

[45] Today, the most walkable and bike friendly communities in U.S. cities have become the most desirable places to live and an increasing number of studies point to the linkage between housing prices and walkability.www.sciencedirect.com/science/article/pii/S0264275114 001474.

[46] A study by Brookings in 2012 of Washington, D.C. neighborhoods revealed that walkable places perform better economically, residents of these areas had more mobility choices and access to transit, walkable places benefit from being near other walkable places, and residents of places with poor walkability were generally less affluent and had less educational attainment. www.brookings.edu/~/media/Research/Files/Papers/2012/5/25-walkable-places-leinberger/25- walkable-places-leinberger.pdf.

[47] See: www.seaholm.info.

[48] See: www.tbpm.org.

[49] See: www.whitehouse.gov/administration/eop/ostp/pcast/docsreports.

[50] See: breatheproject.org/learn/breathe-cam.

[51] See, for example: www.datadrivendetroit.org/webftp/Project Docs/StateOfTheEnvironment/Health/AsthmaZipCode0709Tricounty.pdf; www.health.ny.gov/statistics/ny asthma.

[52] See: air.propellerhealth.com.

[53] The Array of Things project is funded through multiple National Science Foundation (NSF) awards totaling $3.25 million along with multiple internal grants from Argonne National Laboratory and the University of Chicago. It includes over $1 million of cost-sharing from the City of Chicago and industry partners. Arrayofthings.github.io.

[54] See: www.ghgprotocol.org/city-accounting.

[55] See: www.compactofmayors.org.

[56] See: www.city-journal.org/2014/24 2 ny-reckless-driving.html.

[57] See: www.visionzeroinitiative.com.

[58] See: saferoutes.lacity.org.

[59] See: Govtech.com/public-safety/New-York-City-Fights-Fire-with-Data.html.

[60] Peter Marx, Chief Technology Officer, City of Los Angeles, personal communication, January, 2016.

[61] See: dpw.lacounty.gov/epd/swims/Residents/franchiseAreas.aspx.

[62] See: news.xerox.com/news/Xerox-CitySight-Data-Analytics-Solution-Helps-Parking-Enforcement-Officers.

[63] See: envisioncharlotte.com.

[64] Amanda Erickson, "A brief history of the birth of urban planning," *The* Atlantic, 2012. www.citylab.com/work/2012/08/brief-history-birth-urban-planning/2365.

[65] See: www-personal.umich.edu/~sdcamp/up540/timeline12.html.

[66] See: www.planningaccreditationboard.org/index,php?id=30.

[67] Michael Batty "Urban Informatics and Big Data," 2013. www.spatialcomplexity.info/files/2015/07/Urban-Informaticsand-Big-Data.pdf.

[68] See: www.wisc.warwick.ac.uk/training/doctoral-training-programme; www.tmu.ac.jp/english/academics/graduate/ues/cus.html and www.citysciences.com.

[69] See: www.northeastern.edu/cssh/policyschool/graduate-programs/urban-informatics.

[70] See: cusp.nyu.edu.

[71] See: www.bartlett.ucl.ac.uk/casa.

[72] "Making sense of the New Urban Science," *Rudin Center*, 2015. www.citiesofdata.org/wp-content/uploads/2015/04/Making-Sense-of-the-New-Science-of-Cities-FINAL-2015.7.7.pdf.

[73] See: senseable.mit.edu.

[74] See: www.santafe.edu/research/cities-scaling-and-sustainability and www.urbanccd.org.

[75] See: cp.media.mit.edu/city-simulation.

[76] The LEED exams are ANSI 17024 accredited; see: ansi.org/news publications/news story.aspx?menuid=7&articleid=8169400a-20f7-491c-872e-fd164ceaee15. For general perspective on ANSI, see: www.ansi.org.

[77] See: www.usgbc.org/articles/leed-facts.

[78] See: ecodistricts.org/certification/protocol.

[79] See: www.whitehouse.gov/sites/default/files/microsites/ostp/PCAST/PCAST worforce edIT Oct-2014.pdf.

[80] See: energy.gov/sites/prod/files/2014/12/f19/Dept%20of%20Commerce%20and%20Dept%20of%20Energy%20Joint%20China% 20Mission%20Statement.pdf.

[81] See: www.nist.gov/cps/sagc.cfm.

[82] See: www.eda.gov/news/blogs/2015/08/20/SC2-Economic-Visioning-Challenge.htm.

[83] See: www.eda.gov/oie/ris.

[84] See: www.challenge.gov/challenge/city-software-development-kit-sdk-data-solutions-challenge.

[85] See: www.transportation.gov/smartcity#sthash.2sp9IzfD.dpuf.

[86] See: www.transportation.gov/ladders.

[87] See: www.transportation.gov/tiger.

[88] See: www.fhwa.dot.gov/ipd/tifia.

[89] See: www.sustainablecommunities.gov.

[90] See: www.whitehouse.gov/the-press-office/2015/07/15/fact-sheet-connecthome-coming-together-ensure-digitalopportunity-all.

[91] See: www.hudexchange.info/programs/sci.

[92] See: portal.hud.gov/hudportal/HUD?src=/press/press releases media advisories/2015/HUDNo 15-079.

[93] See: portal.hud.gov/idc/groups/public/documents/document/renew300.pdf.pdf.

[94] See: www.whitehouse.gov/the-press-office/2014/01/08/fact-sheet-president-obama-s-promise-zones-initiative.

[95] There is ample history of public policy efforts to creating enabling districts—for example, both Presidents Reagan and Clinton experimented with Enterprise Zones—with programs varying in their emphasis on process v. outcomes. www.house.leg.state.mn.us/hrd/pubs/entzones.pdf.

[96] See: portal.hud.gov/hudportal/HUD?src=/program offices/public indian housing/programs/ph/programs.

[97] See: betterbuildingssolutioncenter.energy.gov/sites/default/files/news/attachments/DOE BB 2015 Progress Report Solution Center.pdf.

[98] See: energy.gov/eere/cities-leading-through-energy-analysis-and-planning.

[99] See: www.epa.gov/wifia/learn-about-water-infrastructure-finance-and-innovation-act-program.

[100] See: www.epa.gov/waterfinancecenter.

[101] See: www.epa.gov/brownfields.

[102] See: www.whitehouse.gov/the-press-office/2015/09/14/fact-sheet-administration-announces-new-smart-citiesinitiative-help.

[103] See: www.us-ignite.org.

[104] See: www.nitrd.gov.

[105] See: www.nitrd.gov/sccc.

[106] See: www.socrata.com.

[107] See: aws.amazon.com/stateandlocal.

[108] See: www.nlc.org/find-city-solutions.

[109] U.S. Department of Transportation Research Data Exchange www.its-rde.net.

[110] Examples include Rockefeller Foundation's 100 Resilient Cities (www.100 resilientcities.org/#/-/) and Bloomberg's What Works Cities (whatworkscities. bloomberg.org)

[111] By contrast, anecdotal reports from city officials point to the challenge of being locked into single-vendor, interoperable systems.

[112] See: www.iso.org/iso/home/standards/management-standards/iso 9000.htm.

[113] See: www.iso.org/iso/news.htm?refid=Ref1848.

[114] See: standards.sae.org/j3016 201401.

[115] See: www.nhtsa.gov/About+NHTSA/Press+Releases/U.S.+Department+of+Transportation+Releases+Policy+on+Automated+Vehi cle+Development.

[116] See: www.citysdk.eu/about-the-project.

[117] See: www.adb.org/publications/managing-asian-cities.

[118] See: chinabusinessreview.com/chinas-green-building-future.

[119] See: www.mckinsey.com/insights/sustainability/building the cities of the future with green districts.

[120] See: www.gov.uk/government/collections/future-of-cities.

[121] Canada also hosts such examples as Zibi, 37-acres of industrial land between (and crossing the boundaries of) the cities of Ottawa and Gatineau in Ontario. It is a brownfield, mixed-use development optimized for hyper-local living and a 90% walkability score, in which any resident can easily walk to their place of work, home of residence or leisure activities. 12% of the Master Planned area is dedicated to public space, transformed from old industrial space. www.zibi.ca.

[122] See: www.governing.com/gov-data/transportation-infrastructure/walk-to-work-cities-map.html.

[123] See: En.wikipedia.org/wiki/List of U.S. cities with most pedestrian commuters.

[124] See: www.census.gov/hhes/commuting/files/2014/acs-25.pdf and kk.sites.itera.dk/apps/kk pub2/pdf/823 Bg65v7UH2t.pdf.

[125] See: www.transportation.gov/smartcity.

[126] See: www.whitehouse.gov/ready-to-work.

[127] See: www.whitehouse.gov/issues/technology/techhire.

[128] See: www.whitehouse.gov/sites/default/files/docs/job-driven training and apprenticeship progress report.pdf.

[129] See: www.whitehouse.gov/sites/default/files/microsites/ostp/PCAST/PCAST worforce edIT Oct-2014.pdf.

[130] See: www.w3.org.

[131] See: www.ietf.org.

[132] See: www.nitrd.gov/sccc.

[133] See: www.codeforamerica.org.

[134] See: datadrivendetroit.org.

[135] See: metrolab.heinz.cmu.edu.

[136] See: www.whitehouse.gov/open.

[137] See: playbook.cio.gov/#play13.

[138] See: handbook.agilegovleaders.org.

[139] See: github.com/usds/playbook/blob/gh-pages/ includes/techfar-online.md#shared-goals-of-modular-contracting-andagile-software-development.

[140] See: socrata.com.

[141] See: us-city.census.okfn.org.

[142] See: www.codeforamerica.org/blog/2014/02/27/mapping-the-open-data-landscape (accessed January 2016).

[143] See: www.openstreetmap.org.

[144] See: www.photogrammetry.com.

[145] See: www.open311.org.

[146] See: en.wikipedia.org/wiki/3-1-1.

[147] See: www.programmableweb.com/news/45-transit-apis-yahoo-traffic-smsmybus-and-bart/2012/02/14.

[148] See: transitapp.com.

[149] See: www.apitools.com/apis/ba-bike-share.

[150] See: developers.google.com/maps/?hl=en.

[151] See: msdn.microsoft.com/en-us/library/hh441725.aspx.

[152] See: wiki.openstreetmap.org/wiki/API.

[153] See: www.programmableweb.com/api/digitalglobe-maps.

[154] See: github.com/developmentseed/landsat-api.

[155] See: developer.nrel.gov/docs/solar.

[156] See: www.zillow.com/howto/api/APIOverview.htm.

[157] See: developer.trulia.com.

[158] See: www.walkscore.com/professional/api.php.

[159] These statistical predictions rely on algorithms that examine spatial and temporal factors from sources such as 911 calls, previous crimes, Census data, and other sources such as public social media, weather, or public transit-vehicle locations and extrapolate these trends towards probable crime hot-spots. While the true usefulness of these approaches is yet to be proven, patterns of burglary have been shows to be relatively predictable; possibly criminals require knowledge of places to be effective.

[160] Questions of whether such strategies can promote strategic behavior on the part of violators, or improve quality of life in target neighborhoods (e.g., subject to greater policing focus) must continue to be explored.

[161] See: datala.github.io/bradley-tower.

[162] See: open.dataforcities.org.

[163] See PCAST report "Big Data: A Technological Perspective," released May 2014. www.whitehouse.gov/sites/default/files/microsites/ostp/PCAST/pcast big data and privacy - may 2014.pdf.

[164] See: www.nitrd.gov.

[165] See: www.whitehouse.gov/the-press-office/2015/07/29/executive-order-creating-national-strategic-computinginitiative.

[166] Early models, such as TRANSIMS from Los Alamos National Laboratory, created a replica of a real city's built environment (buildings, roads, public spaces) and, as the name indicates, were principally models of traffic flow. Later developments used these integrated models to simulate epidemic outbreaks (such as influenza) and for scenario generation.

[167] See: www.cdc.gov/asthma/asthmadata.htm.

[168] See: www.nerdwallet.com/blog/health/diseases/asthma-best-place-to-live.

[169] See: www.hopkinsmedicine.org/news/media/releases/time to rethink the inner city asthma epidemic.

[170] See: www.npr.org/sections/health-shots/2015/01/20/378608279/the-inner-city-might-not-be-to-blame-for-highasthma-rates.

[171] See: datasmart.ash.harvard.edu/news/article/monitoring-air-quality-and-the-impacts-of-pollution-679.

[172] See: www.forbes.com/sites/athenahealth/2015/12/07/how-one-city-is-fighting-asthma-and-saving-money.

[173] See: www.nyc.gov/html/nycha/downloads/pdf/hud-asthma-release-2.pdf.

[174] See: www.downstate.edu/bhr/reports/Brooklyn-Health-Report-Asthma-2.pdf.

[175] See: www.datadrivendetroit.org/webftp/ProjectDocs/StateOfTheEnvironment/Health/Asthma ZipCode0709 Tri county.pdf.

[176] See: air.propellerhealth.com.

[177] See: Arrayofthings.github.io.

[178] See: www.link.nyc.

[179] O'Brien and. Sampson. "Public and private spheres of neighborhood disorder: Assessing pathways to violence using large-scale digital records." *Journal of Research in Crime and Delinquency*, 2015. dash.harvard.edu/bitstream/handle/1/17553309/JRCD O'Brien Sampson%202015.pdf?sequence=3.

[180] Alexander Slagg. "Chicago leverages 311 and big data to tackle its rat problems," StateTech, 2014. www.statetechmagazine.com/article/204/11/chicago-leverages-311-and-big-data-tackle-its-rat-problems.

[181] Michael Bloomberg, "What Paris talks have accomplished so far," *BloombergView*, 2015. www.bloombergview.com/articles/2015-12-06/what-paris-talks-have-accomplished-so-far.

[182] "21 U.S. cities will measure, disclose CO2 emissions," *ReliablePlant. www.reliableplant.com/Read/12980/21-us-citieswill-measure,-disclose-co2-emissions.*

[183] See: www.ghgprotocol.org/city-accounting.

[184] See: www.compactofmayors.org.

[185] See: www.compactofmayors.org/resources/tools-for-cities.

[186] See: www.city-journal.org/2014/24 2 ny-reckless-driving.html.

[187] See: www.visionzeroinitiative.com.

[188] See: saferoutes.lacity.org.

[189] See: Govtech.com/public-safety/New-York-City-Fights-Fire-with-Data.html.

[190] See: www1.nyc.gov/site/analytics/meet-team.page.

[191] Peter Marx, Chief Technology Officer, City of Los Angeles, personal communication, January, 2016.

[192] See: harris.uchicago.edu.

[193] See: www.fastcompany.com/3051578/elasticity/hitachi-says-it-can-predict-crimes-before-they-happen.

[194] See: www.chicagomag.com/city-life/January-2016/The-Answer-My-Friend.

[195] See: energy.gov/sites/prod/files/2014/12/f19/Dept%20of%20Commerce%20and%20Dept%20of%20Energy%20Joint%20China% 20Mission%20Statement.pdf.

[196] See: www2.ntia.doc.gov.

[197] See: www.nist.gov/cps/sagc.cfm.

[198] See: www.whitehouse.gov/the-press-office/2015/09/14/fact-sheet-administration-announces-new-smart-citiesinitiative-help.

[199] See: www.nist.gov/itl/ssd/cyber-physical-systems.cfm and www.nist.gov/el/nist-releases-draft-framework-cyberphysical-systems-developers.cfm.

[200] See: www.eda.gov/about/investment-programs.htm.

[201] See: www.eda.gov/news/blogs/2015/08/20/SC2-Economic-Visioning-Challenge.htm.

[202] See: www.eda.gov/oie/ris.

[203] See: www.eda.gov/oie/files/ris/2015-RIS-FAQs.pdf.

[204] See: www.eda.gov/news/press-releases/2015/03/30/ris.htm.

[205] See: www.challenge.gov/challenge/city-software-development-kit-sdk-data-solutions-challenge.

[206] See: www.transportation.gov/smartcity#sthash.2sp9IzfD.dpuf.

[207] See: www.transportation.gov/ladders.

[208] See: www.transportation.gov/tiger.

[209] See: www.transportation.gov/sites/dot.gov/files/docs/TIGER PLANNING SUSTAINABLE COMMUNITIES.pdf.

[210] See: www.whitehouse.gov/the-press-office/2015/07/15/fact-sheet-connecthome-coming-together-ensure-digitalopportunity-all.

[211] See: www.hudexchange.info/programs/sci.

[212] See: portal.hud.gov/hudportal/HUD?src=/press/press releases media advisories/2015/ HUDNo 15-079.

[213] See: www.hudexchange.info/news/office-of-economic-resilience-update-april-28-2015.

[214] See: portal.hud.gov/idc/groups/public/documents/document/renew300.pdf.pdf.

[215] See: www.whitehouse.gov/the-press-office/2015/07/07/fact-sheet-administration-announces-new-initiative-increasesolar-access.

[216] See: blog.hud.gov/index.php/2015/07/20/powering-a-brighter-future-in-public-housing.

[217] See: www.whitehouse.gov/the-press-office/2014/01/08/fact-sheet-president-obama-s-promise-zones-initiative.

[218] There is ample history of public policy efforts to creating enabling districts—for example, both Presidents Reagan and Clinton experimented with Enterprise Zones—with programs varying in their emphasis on process v. outcomes. www.house.leg.state.mn.us/wrd/pubs/endzones.pdf.

[219] See: portal.hud.gov/hudportal/HUD?src=/program offices/public indian housing/programs/ph/programs.

[220] See: resources.hud.gov.

[221] See: betterbuildingssolutioncenter.energy.gov/sites/default/files/news/attachments/DOE BB 2015 Progress Report Solution Center.pdf.

[222] See: www.nrel.gov/docs/fy15osti/64128.pdf.

[223] See: energy.gov/eere/cities-leading-through-energy-analysis-and-planning.

[224] "City-Level Energy Decision Making: Data Use in Energy Planning, Implementation, and Evaluation in U.S. Cities," *NREL/TP-7A40-64128*, 2015. www.nrel.gov/docs/fy15osti/64128.pdf.

[225] See: www3.epa.gov/environmentaljustice.

[226] See: www.epa.gov/wifia/learn-about-water-infrastructure-finance-and-innovation-act-program.

[227] See: www.epa.gov/waterfinancecenter.

[228] See: www.epa.gov/cwsrf.

[229] See: www.epa.gov/drinkingwatersrf.

[230] See: www.epa.gov/green-infrastructure/green-infrastructure-collaborative.

[231] See: www3.epa.gov/environmentaljustice.

[232] See: www.epa.gov/brownfields.

[233] See: www.whitehouse.gov/the-press-office/2015/09/14/fact-sheet-administration-announces-new-smart-citiesinitiative-help.

[234] See: www.nitrd.gov/sccc.

[235] See: www.masdar.ae.

[236] See: amsterdamsmartcity.com.

[237] See: actua.ad/en/#.

[238] See: smartcity.bcn.cat/en.

[239] See: www.mohurd.gov.cn.

[240] See: www.hcu-hamburg.de/research/citysciencelab.

[241] See: www.smartcitieschallenge.in.

[242] See: www.sparktherise.com/home.

[243] See: songdoibd.com.

[244] See: www.mksmart.org.

[245] See: ts.catapult.org.uk.

[246] See: www.pmo.gov.sg/smartnation.

[247] See: lkycic.sutd.edu.sg.

[248] See: smart.mit.edu.

[249] See: international.stockholm.se/city-development/the-smart-city.

[250] See: www.chinapost.com.tw/taiwan/business/2016/01/11/455759/MIT-team.htm.

[251] See: oats.org.

In: Technology and the Future of Cities
Editor: Diana L. Washington
ISBN: 978-1-53610-418-9

Chapter 2

FACT SHEET: ADMINISTRATION ANNOUNCES NEW "SMART CITIES" INITIATIVE TO HELP COMMUNITIES TACKLE LOCAL CHALLENGES AND IMPROVE CITY SERVICES*

Office of the Press Secretary

"Every community is different, with different needs and different approaches. But communities that are making the most progress on these issues have some things in common. They don't look for a single silver bullet; instead they bring together local government and nonprofits and businesses and teachers and parents around a shared goal."

– President Barack Obama

Today, the Administration is announcing a new "Smart Cities" Initiative that will invest over $160 million in federal research and leverage more than 25 new technology collaborations to help local communities tackle key challenges such as reducing traffic congestion, fighting crime, fostering economic growth, managing the effects of a changing climate, and improving the delivery of city services. The new initiative is part of this Administration's

* This is an edited, reformatted and augmented version of a fact sheet issued by the White House, September 14, 2015.

overall commitment to target federal resources to meet local needs and support community-led solutions.

Over the past six years, the Administration has pursued a place-based approach to working with communities as they tackle a wide range of challenges, from investing in infrastructure and filling open technology jobs to bolstering community policing. Advances in science and technology have the potential to accelerate these efforts. An emerging community of civic leaders, data scientists, technologists, and companies are joining forces to build "Smart Cities" – communities that are building an infrastructure to continuously improve the collection, aggregation, and use of data to improve the life of their residents – by harnessing the growing data revolution, low-cost sensors, and research collaborations, and doing so securely to protect safety and privacy.

As part of the initiative, the Administration is announcing:

- More than $35 million in new grants and over $10 million in proposed investments to build a research infrastructure for Smart Cities by the National Science Foundation and National Institute of Standards and Technology.
- Nearly $70 million in new spending and over $45 million in proposed investments to unlock new solutions in safety, energy, climate preparedness, transportation, health and more, by the Department of Homeland Security, Department of Transportation, Department of Energy, Department of Commerce, and the Environmental Protection Agency.
- More than 20 cities participating in major new multi-city collaborations that will help city leaders effectively collaborate with universities and industry.

Today, the Administration is also hosting a White House Smart Cities Forum, coinciding with Smart Cities Week hosted by the Smart Cities Council, to highlight new steps and brainstorm additional ways that science and technology can support municipal efforts.

The Administration's Smart Cities Initiative will begin with a focus on key strategies:

- *Creating test beds for "Internet of Things" applications and developing new multi-sector collaborative models*: Technological advancements and the diminishing cost of IT infrastructure have created the potential for an "Internet of Things," a ubiquitous network of connected devices, smart sensors, and big data analytics. The United States has the opportunity to be a global leader in this field, and cities represent strong potential test beds for development and deployment of Internet of Things applications. Successfully deploying these and other new approaches often depends on new regional collaborations among a diverse array of public and private actors, including industry, academia, and various public entities.

- *Collaborating with the civic tech movement and forging intercity collaborations*: There is a growing community of individuals, entrepreneurs, and nonprofits interested in harnessing IT to tackle local problems and work directly with city governments. These efforts can help cities leverage their data to develop new capabilities. Collaborations across communities are likewise indispensable for replicating what works in new places.
- *Leveraging existing Federal activity*: From research on sensor networks and cybersecurity to investments in broadband infrastructure and intelligent transportation systems, the Federal government has an existing portfolio of activities that can provide a strong foundation for a Smart Cities effort.
- *Pursuing international collaboration*: Fifty-four percent of the world's population live in urban areas. Continued population growth and urbanization will add 2.5 billion people to the world's urban population by 2050. The associated climate and resource challenges demand innovative approaches. Products and services associated with this market present a significant export opportunity for the U.S., since almost 90 percent of this increase will occur in Africa and Asia.

Complementing this effort, the President's Council of Advisors on Science and Technology is examining how a variety of technologies can enhance the future of cities and the quality of life for urban residents. The Networking and Information Technology Research and Development (NITRD) Program is also announcing the release of a new framework to help coordinate Federal agency investments and outside collaborations that will guide foundational research and accelerate the transition into scalable and replicable Smart City approaches. Finally, the Administration's growing work in this area is reflected in the Science and Technology Priorities Memo, issued by the Office of Management and Budget and Office of Science and Technology Policy in preparation for the President's 2017 budget proposal, which includes a focus on cyber-physical systems and Smart Cities.

Key Steps by the Administration Being Announced Today

Building a Research Infrastructure for Smart Cities

The National Science Foundation (NSF) is announcing over $35 million in Smart Cities-related grants and planning new investments in FY16. With a new foundation-wide effort devoted to Smart and Connected Communities, NSF will bring academic researchers and community stakeholders together to unlock transformational progress on important challenges — including health and wellness, energy efficiency, building automation, transportation, and public safety — through research to integrate new digital tools and engineering solutions into the physical world. NSF announcements in support of this agenda include:

- $11.5 million in new awards to develop and scale next-generation Internet application prototypes that leverage gigabit speeds to achieve transformative impact in areas ranging from health care to public safety. These investments include new awards to US Ignite, Inc., and the Mozilla Foundation to create "Living Labs," or communities of practice that facilitate the participation of citizens and community organizations, as well as idea and application sharing, across cities and regions. US Ignite is a public-private collaboration spanning over 40 cities and communities across the Nation. The Mozilla Foundation is a nonprofit dedicated to promoting openness, innovation, and participation on the Internet.
- $10 million in new Cyber-Physical Systems Program research awards focused on Smart and Connected Communities. These awards support research in the integration of computing, networking, and physical systems, such as in self-driving cars and smart buildings. The research awards being announced today help to establish the foundation for Smart Cities and the "Internet of Things." One such award, to Kansas State University, will fund research on novel approaches to integrate distributed power sources, such as rooftop solar panels and storage batteries, with the existing electric power grid.
- $7.5 million in proposed FY16 spending for urban science that will support research that integrates advanced digital tools with the physical world to improve quality of life, health and wellbeing, and learning in communities.

- $4 million to support academic-industry collaborations to translate innovative research and emerging technologies into smart service systems, such as smart energy services and on-demand transportation.
- $3 million for the University of Chicago to support the creation of the Array of Things in Chicago, the first such network to serve as an infrastructure for researchers to rapidly deploy sensors, embedded systems, computing, and communications systems at scale in an urban environment. Comprised of 500 nodes deployed throughout the city of Chicago, each with power, Internet, and a base set of sensing and embedded information systems capabilities, the Array of Things will continuously measure the physical environment of urban areas at the city block scale and unlock promising new research trajectories.
- $2.5 million for researchers to participate in the 2015 NIST Global City Teams Challenge, which supports "high-risk, high-reward" research on the effective integration of networked computing systems and physical systems to meet community challenges.
- $2.5 million in new research awards to support improvements in the design and operation of interdependent critical infrastructure, such as electrical power and transportation systems, ensuring they are resilient to disruptions and failures from any cause.
- $2 million in new Smart and Connected Health research awards with a focus on Smart and Connected Communities. The awards being announced today will support the development of next-generation health care solutions that leverage sensor technology, information and machine learning technology, decision support systems, modeling of behavioral and cognitive processes, and more.
- A new Dear Colleague Letter encouraging Early-Concept Grants for Exploratory Research proposals, as well as supplemental proposals to existing grants, to grow a Smart and Connected Communities research community and pilot early-stage efforts.

The National Institute of Standards and Technology (NIST) plans to invest $5 million in Smart Cities in FY16 and is launching a new round of the Global City Teams Challenge. Proposed FY16 investments will foster collaborations with communities and industry to demonstrate the capabilities of Internet of Things technologies to benefit local communities, while developing related performance standards and measurement tools. In addition, NIST is launching the next round of its Global City Teams Challenge (GCTC), using a new approach that will challenge teams of cities to set Smart City goals and then work with innovators to develop, deploy, and evaluate standards-based Smart City technologies that measurably improve residents' quality of life. The private sector is stepping up as well, including:

- IBM is announcing it will organize GCTC 2016 kick off events in an additional 30 cities in Asia Pacific, Latin America, North America, Europe, Middle East, and Africa. It will also provide technology experts to mentor and educate the worldwide participants in agile Internet of Things applications, design, and development throughout the GCTC 2016 challenge.
- AT&T is announcing that it will support Internet of Things and Smart Cities technology adoption by supporting testbeds in cities in the U.S. and globally. AT&T will select 10 U.S. cities to deploy technology for smart metering, lighting, traffic management, parking, and public safety. The company will host a Smart Cities hackathon with NIST participation at the AT&T Developer Summit in January 2016 with participating cities.

Unlocking New Solutions for National Priorities

The Department of Homeland Security (DHS) is announcing plans to invest $50 million over five years to develop cutting-edge emergency response technologies for Smart Cities. Through the Next Generation First Responder Apex Program, the DHS Science and Technology Directorate is developing and integrating innovative technologies to ensure first responders are protected, connected, and fully aware – helping to better prepare them for threats and disasters of all sizes. As part of this effort, DHS is also collaborating with NIST to leverage Smart Cities data, analytics, and predictive modeling to give responders the right information at the right time, increasing responder operational efficiency and safety.

The Department of Transportation (DOT) is announcing over $40 million in new funding to advance transportation for Smart Cities, building on a broad base of existing research and outreach to spur the development of next-generation transportation systems, including:

- DOT is announcing awards today of up to $42 million in its first wave of Connected Vehicle Pilots, including $20 million for the installation of this technology in midtown Manhattan, and $17 million to address congestion in downtown Tampa.

- A new funding opportunity of approximately $4 million focused on how mobile telecommunications and travel data integration can make traveling easier and more efficient, as well as how incentives can help promote safer travel. Past research has explored the potential for automated vehicles, dynamic ridesharing, and integration of sensor data to assist navigation for blind and vision impaired pedestrians. This new opportunity from the Federal Highway Administration Exploratory Advanced Research Program will build on these results in further areas related to smart cities.
- Gathering input on integrating vehicle data, technologies, and applications with other systems across a city. On November 4, 2015, the Connected Cities Research Program will hold a public workshop in Washington, DC, to solicit stakeholder input on the connected cities research program structure and its focus areas.
- Advancing outreach and collaboration on connected and automated vehicles. On November 4-5, 2015, the University Transportation Centers (UTC) research program will host a conference on the impact of connected and automated vehicles on transportation – to include, planning, policy, land use, design as well as smart cities areas of interest: operations, freight movements, and transit.

The Department of Energy (DOE) will invest almost $10 million to expand efforts to support the emergence of smart, energy-efficient and low-emission cities that are leveraging Smart Cities technologies. These new steps include:

- Creating a new SMART Mobility consortium, with $5 million in new research funding. DOE will launch a Systems and Modeling for Accelerated Research in Transportation (SMART) Mobility consortium to examine the nexus of energy and mobility for future transportation systems. Initial research will focus on connected and automated vehicles, urban science, decision science, multi-modal transport, and integrated vehicle-fueling infrastructure systems.
- Over $3 million in proposed funding to advance smart building technologies that optimize operational performance, maximize energy savings, and participate in smart communications within buildings, from building to building, and from buildings to the grid. Through the High Impact Technology Catalyst, DOE is proposing to spend more than $3 million over the next three years to accelerate the uptake of nascent market-ready technologies and solutions that support self-

configuring, self-commissioning and self-learning buildings. The Department will also lead a new collaborative effort with multiple private sector groups to leverage the work of the existing Better Buildings Energy Data Accelerator to promote better access to building energy data in new cities across the country.

- A Smart Grid Integration Challenge for Cities, offering at least $1 million in funding. DOE's Office of Electricity Delivery and Energy Reliability will launch a new challenge competition in 2016 to support city efforts to implement sensing, data sharing, and data analytics to achieve city goals for reducing energy consumption. The competition will be open to city governments that have already developed a roadmap or an action plan with clearly defined targets for energy consumption reduction for the entire city.

The Department of Commerce's Economic Development Administration (EDA) is planning a new $10 million round of its Regional Innovation Strategies funding opportunity, with a new focus on catalyzing regionally-grown solutions to communities' most pressing problems. As part of the 2016 Regional Innovation Strategies (RIS) program, which helps build regional capacity to support entrepreneurs and growing young companies, EDA will conduct directed outreach to programs that support early-stage companies that use technologies to solve communities' most pressing problems, such as companies in the Smart Cities sector, which can have a significant positive impact on a community's or region's economic growth and resiliency. As part of the 2017 RIS Program, EDA plans, where appropriations allow, to include the i6 Impact Challenge and the Conscious Seed Fund Support (C-SFS) Grants program, which will support high-growth companies that solve these pressing problems to help make cities and communities smarter and more economically resilient.

The Environmental Protection Agency (EPA) is announcing new steps to unlock Smart Cities approaches to environmental monitoring and analysis. These new steps are designed to help communities undertake innovative sensor-based approaches to improve data collection and analysis of environmental condition and risk, including:

- Up to $4.5 million in new grant funding to conduct innovative air quality pilot studies in several cities using low-cost portable air pollution sensors. The grants will empower communities and individuals with new data to help them understand their air pollution exposure at a more granular level, while improving our understanding and management of data quality from distributed sensors.

- Deployment of EPA's Village Green Project air monitoring stations to pilot test in three new cities over the next year: Oklahoma City, OK, Hartford, CT, and Chicago, IL. Building on four already successful deployments, the Village Green Project enables researchers and citizens to monitor and analyze local air quality, unlocking a better understanding of local variations and air quality trends.
- A new project to create a software module for scenario planning that helps communities plan for health impacts by evaluating the effects of change in the built environment on local public health. By developing a software module that can integrate with open scenario planning tools and evaluate potential consequences, EPA will help communities grow in more sustainable development patterns.

The U.S. Census Bureau (Census) is announcing new steps to expand the open-source CitySDK project, making valuable data available to communities and civic innovators. To help incubate new apps that are based on open data, including Smart Cities apps with broad civic benefits, Census is launching the following:

- A pilot program of data innovation workshops delivered in close collaboration with city experts to help solve the most pressing local issues. Kicking off this fall in North Carolina, the pilot will help bridge the data gap between Federal, state, and city data, and scale nationally through the Census's network of 50 State Data Centers. A key focus of the pilot will be helping cities break down data silos to enable smarter disaster response.
- Releasing an agile playbook for civic innovators, co-developed by Census and Waffle.io. Launching this fall at the 2015 Code for America Summit, the playbook will enable teams of civic hackers to run lean workshops and build Smart City solutions, using open-source tools like CitySDK, Waffle.io, and Github.

New Steps Being Taken by Cities, Universities, Industry, and Others in Response to the Administration's Call to Action.

New Multi-City Collaborations to Support Smart Cities

More than 20 city-university collaborations are launching the MetroLab Network, with more than 60 Smart City projects in the next year. Supported by a newly announced grant of $1 million from the John D. and Catherine T. MacArthur Foundation, the MetroLab Network will leverage university expertise to address challenges facing cities and regions across the country. The Network will provide a platform upon which established and emerging city-university relationships can share successful projects, coordinate multi-city, multi-university research efforts, and compete for research and project funding. The founding members have collectively committed to undertaking more than 60 projects over the next year, which will improve the efficiency and effectiveness of infrastructure and services in our cities and communities and increase the productivity and competitiveness of our regional economies. Communities and their university counterparts signing onto the network with a joint letter to the President include:

- Atlanta, with Georgia State University and Georgia Tech
- Boston, with Boston Area Research Initiative
- Chicago, with the University of Chicago
- Cuyahoga County, with Case Western University
- Dallas, with Texas Research Alliance
- Detroit, with Wayne State University
- Houston, with Rice University
- Madison, with University of Wisconsin-Madison
- Memphis, with University of Memphis
- Minneapolis & St. Paul, with University of Minnesota
- Montgomery County, with University of Maryland and Universities at Shady Grove
- New York City, with New York University
- Philadelphia, with Drexel University and University of Pennsylvania
- Pittsburgh, with Carnegie Mellon University
- Portland, with Portland State University
- Providence, with Brown University, College Unbound, and Rhode Island School of Design
- San Diego, with University of California San Diego
- San Jose, with San Jose State University
- Seattle, with University of Washington
- South Bend, with University of Notre Dame

- Washington, DC, with Howard University, Georgetown University, and George Washington University

Envision America, a new nationwide nonprofit, is issuing a challenge to America's cities to become smarter by accelerating deployment of innovative technologies that tackle energy, water, waste, and air challenges. City leaders from 10 winning communities will participate in Envision America's workshop in January in Charlotte, NC, where they will work with leading experts from industry and academia to diagnose needs, workshop solutions, and develop new smart initiatives for their community. In addition, they will receive technical assistance throughout the year to support the implementation of their plans. Winners will be selected for participation in the Envision America program on the basis of several criteria, including goals, collaborations among local institutions and other stakeholders, and commitment to developing innovative approaches foundational to a Smart City. This effort builds on the cross-sector collaborative model and local results of Envision Charlotte. The new effort is supported by Accelerated Innovations, Autodesk, Bank of America, Cisco, Duke Energy, GE, Itron, Landis+Gyr, Microsoft, and Qualcomm Technologies, Inc. Complementing the Envision America Challenge, supporters are also taking the following steps:

- Accelerated Innovations will equip winning cities with the Envision America app, a community engagement platform built to facilitate, measure and gamify large-scale sustainability action campaigns.
- GE is sponsoring an Envision America Appathon to engage the civic tech community in a collaborative effort to solve city challenges.
- Microsoft is providing each winning city with one year of access to the Microsoft Azure Government cloud platform, with ongoing assistance to develop smart city solutions.

Additional New Steps by Private and Community Leaders

City Digital, a Chicago-based consortium, will launch two pilots focused on major urban infrastructure challenges. These projects, using Chicago as a testbed for technology and demonstration, focus on deploying a network of sensors to gather data on green infrastructure, and a virtual underground mapping platform to detect and monitor underground infrastructure. The inaugural pilots bring together the city, academia as well as corporate members of the City Digital UI Labs collaboration – Microsoft, Accenture, ComEd, Siemens, Tyco and HBK Engineering.

Dallas is launching the Dallas Innovation Alliance. Initial efforts will center in downtown's West End district and focus on infrastructure, mobility and connected living. Led by the Dallas Entrepreneur Center, charter members include Mayor Mike Rawlings, AECOM, AT&T, IBM, Microsoft, Schneider Electric, Dallas Regional Chamber, Dallas Area Rapid Transit, Dallas Convention and Visitor's Bureau, Downtown Dallas Inc., Texas Research Alliance, and The Real Estate Council.

IBM is deploying a Smarter Cities Challenge team in Detroit to help the city and the Detroit Land Bank Authority (DLBA) remove blight and build smarter Detroit neighborhoods. Through this initiative, a team of top IBM experts will spend three weeks helping Mayor Mike Duggan and the DLBA design a strategy for cost-efficient, sustainable removal, recycling and re-use of debris from abandoned and neglected properties, thereby allowing the DLBA to redirect its limited resources to making strategic investments in neighborhoods. The project will also receive a special grant of Twitter data, which will provide analysis of historical and current social media data to help tackle the issue.

The National League of Cities and 25 local governments announce the 2015 winners of the Multi-City Innovation Campaign to support the efforts of civic innovators tackling community challenges**.** The two winners – selected from 10 tech company finalists and voted on by over 20 cities around the country – are Bluelight, a mobile 911 app, and Ride, a tool that helps cities collect and analyze bike data. The winning companies have each agreed to undertake a four-city pilot, which will begin in early 2016.

New York City will create a series of neighborhood innovation labs across the five boroughs. The new labs will accelerate the testing and deployment of new Smart City technologies. Developed by the City's Chief Technology Officer, the Mayor's Office of Technology and Innovation, the NYU Center for Urban Science and Progress (CUSP), and New York City Economic Development Corporation, the neighborhood innovation labs will build on the CUSP Quantified Community research facility and the Mayor's efforts to expand free public Wi-Fi networks across the city, leveraging this connectivity and the Internet of Things to help improve day-to-day life for community residents and small businesses.

Siemens USA will support the Carbon Neutral Cities Alliance (CNCA), an effort launched earlier this year by mayors of 17 international cities across nine nations. By making the Siemens' City Performance Tool available to

CNCA, alliance members will be able to leverage the software model to evaluate how specific building, transport, and energy technologies can help them achieve their environmental goals.

In: Technology and the Future of Cities
Editor: Diana L. Washington
ISBN: 978-1-53610-418-9

Chapter 3

SMART AND CONNECTED COMMUNITIES FRAMEWORK*

The Networking and Information Technology Research and Development Program

VISION AND ACTIONS TO BE TAKEN

This framework outlines a vision and an approach agencies can use to move forward together in pursuing a vision of smart and connected communities. Activities within the framework include the entire pipeline from research and development to deployment of new tech-driven services and infrastructure in cities. The success of the framework requires federal interagency coordination, cooperation with external stakeholders, and next steps planning for Federal action.

Vision

As the result of coordinated Federal action and partnerships with industry, academia, and other government entities, communities in all settings and at all

* This is an edited, reformatted and augmented version of Version 4 of a working document, issued by the The Networking and Information Technology Research and Development (NITRD) Program, November 25, 2015.

scales have access to advanced cyber-physical systems/Internet of Things technologies and services to enhance the sustainability and quality of life, improved health and safety, and economic prosperity for their residents.

Scope

The Cyber-Physical Systems Senior Steering Group (CPS-SSG) will work to coordinate efforts among Federal agency and with public-private partnerships for smart and connected communities. The relevant agency activities include:

- Performing foundational research and accelerating innovation and transition in scalable and replicable smart city solutions
- Applying advanced cyber-physical systems concepts, coupled with sociotechnical system understanding, to integrate city-scale IT and physical infrastructures
- Enabling replicable smart city solutions that provide powerful new safe, reliable, sustainable, resilient, secure, privacy-enhancing, and cost-saving platforms and services
- Promoting discovery, innovation, and entrepreneurship in smart city technologies
- Facilitating the ability of communities to apply cyber-physical systems concepts to solutions that make them more livable, workable, safe, and sustainable and that support an informed and engaged populace

Goals

The goals of the participating agencies under this framework include:

- Creating next-generation capabilities by furthering and leveraging (via fundamental R&D) cyber physical systems, smart systems, sociotechnical systems understanding, and other emerging technologies, processes, and policies
- Supporting the R&D necessary to create smart cities using data analytics to enhance individuals' Quality of Life, to improve their

health and safety, and economic prosperity, to make better decisions and breakthrough discoveries, and to take confident action based on the analytics

- Building and expanding access to the smart and connected communities resources – both domain specific and shared – that are needed for agencies to best achieve their mission goals and for the country to innovate and benefit
- Promoting interoperable, standards-based smart city solutions that reduce deployment costs and enable modular architectures that are flexible and adaptable in meeting a community's needs
- Improving the national landscape for education and training to fulfill increasing demand for both analytical talent and capacity for the broader workforce to support smart and connected communities

The agencies will consider how to create new and enhance existing connections, for example:

- Fostering the creation of new partnerships that cross sectors and domains
- Creating new partnerships that enable the interconnection and interplay of smart cities and technology innovators across agency missions
- Facilitating access to high value innovation, including small cities and rural communities with limited resources
- Ensuring the long-term sustainability and continued development of high-value innovation

The outcomes of activities inspired by the framework include:

- Applications - innovative technology that will enhance sustainable livelihoods, and the quality of life
- Analytics - acquiring information from the social, biological, and physical elements that constitute the environment
- People (smart citizens) - the education and tools necessary to create a smart city workforce and a citizenry able to benefit from smart city solutions

- Partnerships - across federal agencies and with stakeholders in industry, academia, and other government entities to achieve positive outcomes
- Deployments – Pilot and at-scale smart city deployments that demonstrate value, feasibility, sustainability, and resiliency

The benefits to communities from activities enabled by the framework include:

- Economic growth and new jobs in businesses that are globally competitive in smart city technologies
- Increase the safety and mobility of roadway travelers and reduce traffic-related pollution
- Reduced energy consumption in human mobility, in commercial and residential buildings, and in commercial operations
- Faster and more resilient wired and wireless communications
- Improved response and recovery to natural and man-made disasters
- Improved monitoring of air and water quality
- Reduced crime
- Increased private sector investment in new and growing businesses as a result of new services
- Expanded public participation in important decisions, such as planning and zoning
- Increased safety of infrastructure from condition-based monitoring
- Improved healthcare through the connection of emergency services to hospitals and diagnostic equipment

Agency Smart and Connected Communities Goals

Department of Energy (DOE)/Office of Electricity Delivery & Energy Reliability (OE)

- The DOE/OE Cybersecurity for Energy Delivery Systems (CEDS) program is working toward resilient energy delivery systems that are able to survive a cyber incident. This further strengthens smart grid cyber-resiliency, and hence the cyber-resilience of smart cities that rely on critical energy delivery infrastructure.

- Smart Grid Integration Challenge for Cities: The Department of Energy Office of Electricity Delivery and Energy Reliability will launch a new challenge competition for at least $1 million in 2016 to recognize U.S. cities as smart city leaders in implementing sensing, data sharing, and data analytics toward achieving energy consumption reduction targets set by individual cities. The competition will be open to city governments, who have already developed a roadmap or an action plan with clearly defined targets for energy consumption reduction for the entire city. Implementation activities under this competition must involve leveraging such technologies as smart grid, energy management systems for homes/buildings/districts, demand response, renewable energy sources and energy storage on a sufficiently large scale that their performance results can be quantified with respect to attaining the near-term and long-term goal targets for energy consumption reduction for the entire city. Each winning city through this competition will serve as a model for replication in other like cities nationwide.

Department of Transportation (DOT)

Through research and deployment of innovative transportation technologies, drive advances in how we move better:

- Reduce or eliminate deaths and serious injuries among all users of the transportation system – drivers, passengers, cyclists, and pedestrians;
- Increase the reliability and efficiency of the transportation system – for the movement of both people and goods;
- Drive innovation in the development of safe, affordable mobility options for all Americans;
- Increase the service life and optimize the maintenance of transportation structures in a state of good repair;
- Reduce the environmental and energy impacts in the development, operation, and maintenance and use of the transportation system; and
- Increase the resilience of the transportation system to withstand severe weather and climate change impacts.

National Institute of Food and Agriculture (NIFA)

- Increased food and nutritional security through the development of high-output and efficient urban agriculture technologies and systems
- More resilient, robust, and reliable agricultural systems while faced with a changing climate and an increasing global population

National Institutes of Health (NIH)

- Enhance collaboration between researchers, smart citizens, local cities and municipalities and other stakeholders to evaluate the health-related benefits of networked sensors, infrastructure, and computing systems.
- Support research that develops, implements and evaluates health-related cyber physical systems in smart cities with consideration of security, privacy, health disparities and human factors
- Foster the development of interoperability, consensus standards, and evidence-base that will ensure appropriate technologies are safe, effective, and sustainable
- Promote a citizen-centric, data-driven system that embraces personalized health information and care options and is capable of learning

National Institute of Standards and Technology (NIST)

- Through the Global City Teams Challenge, bring together teams of cities and innovators working in partnership to use Internet of Things technologies in improving the safety, sustainability, livability, and workability of communities worldwide.
- Using open, consensus-based public working groups, develop a comprehensive framework for the design, evaluation, and operation of complex cyber-physical systems, including smart city technologies at scale.
- Through the Smart Grid program and public-private Smart Grid Interoperability Panel, work with the private sector on smart grid

interoperability and security standards that enable the intelligent use of energy resources as a key component of smart city solutions.

- Through the National Cybersecurity Center of Excellence (NCCOE), provide businesses with real-world cybersecurity solutions based on commercially available technologies for smart city applications in areas including energy, transportation, and finance.
- Through the Big Data program collaborating with public working group and international standards effort, bring together a reference architecture that is vendor-neutral, technology- and infrastructure-agnostic to enable data scientists to perform analytics processing for their given data sources without worrying about the underlying computing environment.
- Through the NIST Cloud Computing Program (NCCP), provide a foundational cloud architecture and metrics to enable secure storage, transmission and processing of data and services through collaborations with public working groups, industry and international standards efforts.
- Promote the emergence of voluntary, consensus international standards that enable interoperable smart city solutions to speed deployment efforts, increase flexibility and capability, reduce costs, and catalyze the emergence of a vibrant and global smart city technologies market.

National Science Foundation (NSF)

- Bring together academic researchers, industrial and non-profit partners, and local cities, municipalities and regions to integrate data sources and networked computing systems with people, physical devices and infrastructure, and anchor institutions to have an impact on quality of life within communities across health and wellness, energy efficiency, building automation, transportation, etc.
- Support the fundamental research that gives rise to novel sociotechnical approaches enabling increased understanding of how to intelligently and effectively design, adapt, and manage Smart and Connected Communities.

National Aeronautics and Space Administration (NASA)

- Apply collaborative, planning, and scheduling applications to enhance multi-modal Smart Cities traffic flow management systems.
- Help accelerate safe and efficient future UAV operations for Smart Cities services, operations, and new businesses.
- Share and promote next generation verification and validation tools to enable smart city developers with the means to assure high integrity, robust, & interoperable complex systems.

INDEX

A

B

D

E

F

G

H

I

O

P

T

U

V

W

X

Y